FUTSAL

SKILLS, STRATEGIES AND SESSION PLANS

FUTSAL

SKILLS, STRATEGIES AND SESSION PLANS

Michael Skubala & Seth Burkett

THE CROWOOD PRESS

First published in 2022 by
The Crowood Press Ltd
Ramsbury, Marlborough
Wiltshire SN8 2HR

enquiries@crowood.com
www.crowood.com

British Library Cataloguing-in-Publication Data
A catalogue record for this book is available from the British Library.

ISBN 978 0 7198 4127 9

Cover design by Sergey Tsvetkov

Contributors
With thanks to key contributors: Marc Carmona; Graeme Dell; Andrew Reading; Jose Pazos 'Pulpis'; Miguel Rodrigo; Mico Martic; Paul McGuinness; Peter Sturgess; Tiago Polido

Illustrations: Juan Tapia Owens

Dedication
For the rock in my life, Samantha, my beautiful girls Gracie Rose, Amelie Betsy and Imogen Elsie, and the rest of my loving family: thank you for all your love and support – particularly over the last few years. – *Michael Skubala*

For all those coaches who worked so hard to make me better at what I do. – *Seth Burkett*

Typeset by Simon and Sons
Printed and bound in India by Parksons Graphics

CONTENTS

FOREWORD

Futsal demands much from coaches. Preparation, method, rigour, discipline, organisation and creativity are essential requirements. Then there's the knowledge that comes from practice, studies, investigations and publications. Someone who has always possessed the profile to deal with these demands is Michael Skubala.

I met Michael many years ago at the University World Cup. This was a fundamental competition for the growth and affirmation of many young players, an excellent launch pad for many of them, as well as the coaches who were present. This connection to universities informs Michael's vision of the way forward and the steps needed to be taken towards the highest levels.

In addition to his remarkable knowledge of the game and his leadership on the field, Michael stands out for his human quality and his incessant search for knowledge. His leadership skills and competitive spirit are notorious and, in my view, he meets all the conditions to assume himself as the main face of futsal development in the English FA. He was capped dozens of times by the national team and then led the team in many occasions. This background brought him a 'know-how' that makes a difference at the highest level.

I praise the organisation of the following pages of this book. This work contemplates and brings together moments and experiences of those who know and understand

Singing the national anthem before an international fixture.

futsal from the inside. Skubala's ideas, which I know well – and many of which I share – are well structured in a clear way that I'm sure will enlighten lovers and scholars of the sport. In this sense, I consider this book to be a must-read. Anyone who wants to understand the dynamics of the sport has here a valuable record, where the main guidelines of training methodologies are outlined in a simple and objective way. Skubala decodes, in these pages, the magic of futsal, what we are passionate about and constantly challenges us to be better and to discover new ways to innovate and surprise. The charm of the sport is here: finding new strategies to "cheat" the opponent and reap rewards from it.

There is no doubt that this is another very valid contribution that will help toward the growth of knowledge in futsal: a book that perfectly combines the beauty of practice with the richness of theory.

Jorge Braz, Portugal 2022
Two-time UEFA European Championship winner,
World Cup winner and voted 'Best coach in the
world' four times in a row by Futsal Planet

PREFACE

I've been involved in futsal since 2003, following my release from the football academy system. After a playing career where I gained over sixty caps for England and thirty caps for Great Britain Universities, I focused solely on coaching. Soon, an opportunity came to coach the England side, and then manage them. Together, we achieved England's highest world ranking to date. I have now been involved in over 200 international games across football and futsal, which has not only been a great honour and learning experience, but also given me a unique insight into coach education and development.

More recently, I've been working with the England youth football teams. As a futsal coach now focused in a football environment, I bring the concepts and principles that I've learned from a futsal culture and apply them to the 11v11 game. Having the ability to look at the football game in a tactical way, as well as being able to coach 'the games within the game', is a powerful weapon to have when developing talent and performance tactical levels. This is where futsal coaches can bring real performance value to the football ecosystem.

I believe that with all the modern mediums and tactical analysis, coaches are rushing to 11v11 and missing crucial detail around smaller numbers. Football is obsessed with 1v1 individual technical actions that then jump straight up to 11v11. Actually, the biggest benefits to teams could come from smaller numbers, such as 4v4. This is where my twin tracking journey is unique for an English-born coach.

To give you a question as we go through this book: is it easier to create overloads in 11v11 or in futsal?

Now consider that question alongside another: how hard would it be to score in a football game that was 37v37 where the goals were smaller?

Throughout my coaching journey I've been fortunate enough to learn from the world's best futsal and football coaches. Finland national team manager Mico Martic, Benfica manager Jose Pazos ('Pulpis'), FC Barcelona coach Marc Carmona, FA National Youth Developer and former Manchester United youth coach under Sir Alex Ferguson, Paul McGuinness, and former England managers Graeme Dell and Pete Sturgess have all contributed session plans for this book and shared their knowledge along the way.

In addition to reading this book, I recommend for any coach to watch as much futsal as possible, including that of the highest level – even if you only plan to use futsal for the development of football players. The FA Coaching badges are another essential resource to build your knowledge of a game.

To start, think of futsal as a totally different sport to football while realising that the two are closely aligned. Be comfortable in the knowledge that there is plenty to learn – much of which will cross over to football. Futsal is not just another recreational format of football like five-a-side. It is so much more than that. Futsal for me is the best small-sided game for football development there is. And we're about to find out why…

INTRODUCTION

Futsal is often credited as one of the fastest-growing indoor sports in the world. There's a reason for that. The game is fast, furious and fun, capable of enhancing the skills of footballers and providing a pathway for players to represent their futsal club in the UEFA Champions League and their country in the FIFA World Cup. Players can expect to have hundreds of touches in a match, numerous involvements in attacking and defensive actions, more decisions and far less time and space than in football. With the reduced space available, futsal is the equivalent of a 37v37 game of football.

For coaches, the involvement on matchday is incomparable. With anything from forty to eighty substitutions a game, strategic timeouts and a wealth of well-worked set-pieces, the coach has far greater influence on a game of futsal than on football.

THE LAWS

For those new to the sport, futsal is a game played between two teams on a 40×20m (for senior age) indoor or hard court. Although there are up to fourteen players in a matchday squad, teams are allowed five players to be on court at any one time. Typically, this means four outfielders and one goalkeeper, although a unique 'fly goalkeeper' ruling allows a team to essentially play with five outfielders in a powerplay – though with the risk that they leave the goal empty. As in football, each team defends their goal and attempts to score in the opposition's. The game is played to touchlines, with restarts coming from a goalkeeper throw, kick-in or corner. Teams have just four seconds to restart play once the ball is in position, maintaining the speed of the game and reducing time-wasting. If the ball is not back in play after four seconds, possession is turned over by the referee.

Substitutions are continuous, performed in a roll-on, roll-off manner and done through an 'entry gate' that is next to a team's bench.

Futsal: fast, furious, fun, and full of emotion.

Going for goal.

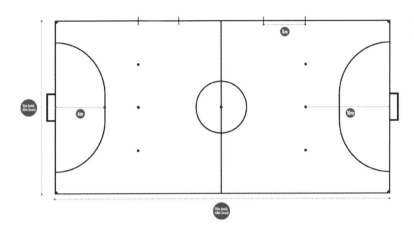

The typical markings of a futsal court.

Substitutes must enter and exit through this gate, clearly marked on the court lines.

Players will typically sub on and off multiple times during a game. Due to the sport's high intensity, players can rarely play for longer than four minutes without requiring rest. A deep squad is therefore highly important for any coach.

To prevent persistent fouling, each team is only allowed to commit five fouls. Every foul after the fifth is punished by a 10m penalty. At half-time, the foul count for both teams resets to zero. The best teams will use their fouls as currency. Fouling an opponent if they are in a dangerous area is an effective tactic so long as it is not the sixth, and certain fouls help teams to maintain intensity against opponents.

There are sometimes misconceptions from social media clips and word of mouth that futsal is for skilful players only. While one-on-one skill is certainly useful, it is ultimately best to have intelligent players who are comfortable anywhere on the court and able to carry out set movements from specific strategies, combining in twos and threes throughout the pitch. To be successful you need to be physical, willing to use your body in intelligent ways.

Because there are fewer players in a smaller space, futsal gives players more fluidity than they'd get from football. This means that players must ultimately do everything in a game. They must defend and attack, while the enhanced fluidity also leads to a greater number of decisions.

THE COACHING FRAMEWORK

Upon first viewing, some may conclude that futsal is a complex game. Others may feel it looks completely random and without tactics. The reality is that futsal is structured in the same way as other sports but with a great ownership on players making their own decisions.

Players must be willing to defend and attack in futsal.

These decisions must be made in the moment due to the speed of the game. Futsal is a high-level technical game, but what sets it apart at the elite standard is the high level of tactics. The real power of futsal is that it is a highly demanding decision-making game.

Teams can have multiple set-piece movements for keeper restarts, kick-ins, corners and free-kicks – all enhanced by the ability to block or screen opponents. They have numerous set rotations, offensive strategies, defensive strategies and formations. The coach's job, then, is to make everything as simple as possible for the player. The coach sets the framework, then allows flexibility through player ownership. This is essential due to the fast nature of the game.

The Golden Rule

Futsal can be complex but that does not mean it needs to be complicated.

Like any invasion game, there are three stages for a futsal player during a game:

- Perception
- Decision
- Action

Perception – What does a player see? What decisions should they make depending on the cues and triggers in any moment of the game?

Decision – What decisions do they make or intend to make depending on what they see?

Action – What do they do?

The coach must support a player in their evolution, providing them with the tools to bring about the correct decision. That decision must ultimately be down to the player; it's impossible to tell a futsal player what to do on court due to the speed of the game. By the time you've opened your mouth, the moment has gone. And once that moment has gone, it's straight onto the next action.

In futsal, the next action is always the most important so there is no time to moan at the referee or teammates, or linger on what has just happened; whether that's a mistake or success. Players must constantly be on the move with high levels of game attention. This not only creates the accountability actions but also behaviours. If you switch off in

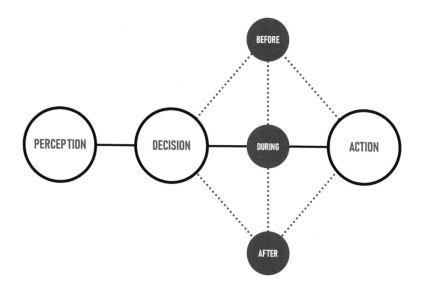

Perception – Decision – Action influences every movement in futsal.

transition you could be scored against within seconds!

In that regard, one golden asset that futsal gives players is instant feedback. If you don't press correctly as a pivot, for example, it could cost your team a goal. This is unlike the eleven-a-side game, where a number 9 in football who doesn't press will not be as severely punished. Accountability for players in futsal in all moments of the game is huge due to the smaller numbers of players on court.

Within the whole perception-decision-action cycle, players must make decisions before they get on the ball, when they are on the ball and after they have played the ball. We must therefore not only coach players on the ball but also off it, both in possession and out of possession. Developing anticipation, decision-making and actions will enable players to react accordingly, almost instantly. This quick, effective reaction of less than one second is the difference between good players and great players. The coach has the ability to influence this hugely.

Ultimately, futsal is a game of space and time and how well you exploit them. By finding and utilizing individual and group space, players will have more time on the ball which will result in better decisions and therefore better actions. The more they understand futsal, and the greater the ownership the coach gives them, the more likely success becomes.

Over the following pages, we want to show you how your players can best utilize space to their benefit and how you as a coach can increase your game understanding. In Chapter 1 we'll help you to build your coaching DNA and game model, allowing you to understand what you're asking of your players and why. Chapter 2 focuses on the principles of in possession play, while Chapter 3 flips the focus to out of possession. Chapter 4 focuses on transitions, which are key moments in futsal matches. From there, Chapter 5 covers special plays unique to futsal, while Chapter 6 discusses set-pieces. Finally, attention turns to one of the most important – if not the most important – positions on the court: the goalkeeper.

Kick-off imminent.

1 BUILDING YOUR DNA AND GAME MODEL

Before any coach analyses their players, they must first analyse themselves. Why did you first get into coaching, and what do you want to achieve within futsal? Perhaps you're a football coach hoping to use futsal to enhance your footballers' game, or maybe you're a national league futsal coach seeking to take your team to the next level. Whatever your background, there are two broad aims that drive the vast majority of coaches: development (improving players) and performance (winning games).

Of course, many coaches will want to develop their players and win games of futsal. However, knowing which of these aims you prioritize will help you to set up your side, manage your team's identity and approach the game with specific tactics (not to say that development does not happen in performance – it just has to be balanced with other priorities). Against a superior side which presses high effectively, for example, do you choose to develop your players by encouraging them to play out from their defensive zone – even if they lose possession and concede goals – in the knowledge that it'll improve their ability to play under pressure despite increasing the team's chances of losing? Or, do you choose to concede possession high up the court, sit in a deep zonal defence and seek to counter-attack when possible, knowing that such tactics will reduce your players' time on the ball and development time in general? The coach will always be balancing these aspects, and the best ones will balance them enough to challenge the players at their disposal.

What do you want from your players?

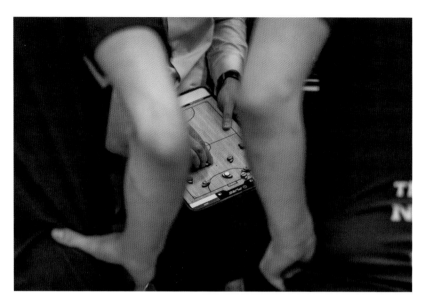

Talking tactics.

Self-analysis does not end there. Understanding your strengths and weaknesses will help you to understand the best way to work with your players, along with the ideal assistants and staff who can complement your coaching style. Even the world's best coaches have weaknesses! Being aware of how to work with them, how to improve them, and how to make sure those weaknesses do not impact your players, is important. Once that awareness is there, action plans can be put in place to turn those weaknesses into strengths. What experiences do you need to have, for example? What tools are available to help you improve? What and where can you learn? When do you want to have improved by and how will you do so? Self-analysis is a constant, with coaching developing with experience and as new ideas come into practice.

In that regard, futsal is an excellent tool for coach development. The coach is central to everything that happens on a futsal court. While a football coach may give guidance from the sidelines during a game and is limited to pre-match and half-time for tactical input with the whole team, the futsal coach can sub players on and off whenever they like during a match to give tactical input and is also allowed to call one strategic timeout each half. Substitutions are unlimited, and coaches often choose to sub their entire team at once (known in the game as a 'Russian four' or 'quartet') to disrupt their opponents tactically, but also to give important tactical guidance to a set group of players. Each 'four' can have a set strategy, changing the flow of the game with each substitution. As coaches can select up to fourteen

Futsal success relies on the capabilities and togetherness of the entire squad.

players in a matchday squad, there is scope to have a varied squad with diverse talents.

With just five players on court at any one time, every tactical tweak has a far greater impact than in a typical football match. Assessing these tweaks will help you to improve as a coach, enabling you to better service your players. The game gives constant and rapid feedback for players and coaches alike.

Looking at the game in minute detail and learning through trial and error allows for effective development. How should your players take advantage of 1v1s or 2v2s, for example, rather than always focusing on overloads?

Once self-analysis is engrained as coach, it's time to also understand what you have to work with.

UNDERSTANDING YOUR PLAYERS

All futsal players are not created equal. Each player has a different journey. Each has their own personal armoury of skill, their strengths and their weaknesses. It is down to you as the coach to make the most of what you have to work with, choosing how you develop the players at your disposal and ensuring they work well together. Make their strengths the team's strengths.

As such a tactical game, the level of experience of your players will naturally dictate the approach you take. While beginners need most work around basic technical concepts such as control, passing, moving, feinting and shooting, developing skills such as the toe-poke and the scoop pass, advanced players need to work more on high-level concepts such as pressing, blocking and 4-0 rotations. Elite players, meanwhile, must master their decision-making, mentality, game effectiveness and reaction times.

For players to develop and perform at the top level they must be competent at individual actions and tactical capabilities, paired actions and capabilities and working in threes. All these

concepts and capabilities fit into any team system, which then underpin team strategy decisions. This is why futsal has been developing footballers for many decades. Rather than seeing futsal as a different sport, in countries like Brazil futsal is simply the small-sided game of choice that all players need to pass through to become competent footballers or futsal players. Indeed, it could be argued that the informal pick-up games seen in the streets of countries like Brazil more closely resemble futsal than football due to the reduced time and space, along with the use of toe-pokes, sole controls, use of the body and creation of overloads, amongst others.

This is illustrated by the futsal development pyramid, which incorporates futsal's threshold concepts.

In the concepts, the higher the level and stage of player, the more focused training becomes on game strategies as a team, rather than an individual. Every player must come through the pyramid from the bottom up. Without the foundation levels of the pyramid, it is challenging to work on the team tactics and game strategies needed for success. However, even older players need to get better at working in pairs, threes or fours (the 'games within the game'). Some concepts cross over between football and futsal, such as inverted full backs and three in a line – both of which are championed by innovative coaches such as Pep Guardiola.

Inverting the Pyramid

The futsal development pyramid shows why domestic structures are so important to international success.

Good players will operate well in these concepts and be adaptable to a team system or strategy.

The futsal development pyramid is key for player development in futsal and football and is a great reference point for where players

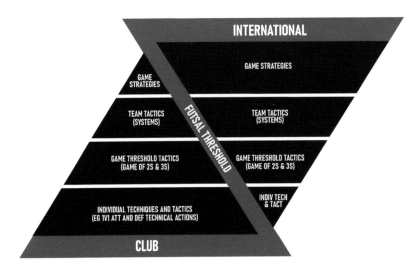

The futsal development pyramid.

are. For example, Paul McGuinness talks about the 1v1 capabilities of players using his own quadrant tool as a model for coaches to see and improve individual game qualities within the perception phase, decision phase and execution phase. This is in relation to individual capabilities such as timing, disguise, positioning, movement, technique and scanning.

Of course, understanding your players does not just relate to their on-court performance.

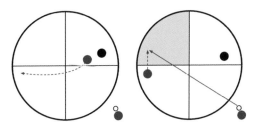

Paul McGuinness's quadrant tool can be used to showcase individual capabilities that create space and opportunities for players.

Dominating Dualities

Timing, disguise, positioning, movement, technique and scanning are not just individual capabilities. They should be done with and without the ball, and should be connected to other players – either in dualities, threes or fours. Any player can improve this part of their game – either in recognition or perception of the situation. These 'games within the game' should be a staple part of any futsal player's diet. The more they practise with teammates, the stronger the chemistry between the two will become.

These movements – often paired – between them and others can be vertical or horizontal. Many of the combinations can be found in all systems of play in the futsal development pyramid. The better that players are at individual, paired and threes connections, the more adaptable they will be to different systems and the higher they are likely to rise up the futsal development pyramid. They will begin to understand little details about their teammates – where and how they like to receive the ball, what options to offer them, what movements do they tend to make – that enhance individual and collective performance.

16

Understanding them from social, technical, physical and psychological aspects is equally as important.

Once you begin to build up an idea of the players you have to work with – in addition to your own self-analysis – it is time to build your tactical game model.

BUILDING YOUR GAME MODEL

A game model helps players and coaching staff alike understand **why** you as a team do what you do, **who** you are as a team (your identity) and **how** you play. These are the foundations upon which all great teams are built. If players don't understand why they're being asked to carry out a certain action, your game model will fundamentally break down.

There are many ways to build a game model and it can be done with or without taking the players into account. For example, you might have a game model that you take into every coaching role that you have, or you may have a model that you build depending on the players you have available. Both approaches are valid.

In the game model, similar to the one used by the England national futsal team, there are three core objectives set in possession and three core objectives set out of possession.

At the core of the game model lies Allen Wade's original football principles of play, which can be split into five main objectives for in possession and five for out of possession. Also included in the game model are the moments of the game, phases of the game, court (or pitch) references, principles of play and sub principles of play, which will be discussed in the upcoming chapters.

There is no one correct game model and this is just one example. Some coaches and teams may prioritize other parts of the game. Remember, a game model is always based on **your** coaching DNA, sometimes on **your** players and **your** team and occasionally even the organisation you work for.

At the heart of any game model, however, are the principles that are the exact same principles of any invasion game. This is why a futsal game model can relate so closely to a football game model. If you are seeking to use futsal to develop football players, then it is worth placing your game models side-by-side and assessing how they can walk and talk in combination with each other.

Whatever the reason for your game model, you should always refer back to it when improving your players. The reason I designed a game model in such a way is that I believe the game not only has cycles within it, but also layers in which we need the players to understand and apply themselves. So building a game model in such a way allowed me to review the learning of the sub principles right the way back to the core of the model and invasion game principles of play. This then helped me with tactical periodization, planning and reviewing sessions and approaching games with a real laser focus and total attention-to-detail.

MOMENTS OF THE GAME

Games are built around moments, and what players do in those moments is key. In futsal, these moments can be split into four distinct categories: in possession, out of possession, positive transition and negative transition. Set-plays and special plays represent sub-categories within the possession phases.

The game of futsal is constantly in flux, with situations quickly changing. Due to the high turnover and unique rules, teams can move between the categories rapidly. It is important to be aware of these moments so that you can plan training and matches around each one. Is there a moment in which your team is particularly strong, for example? What can you do to capitalize on each of these?

There is no special formula for which moment will occur at any time. Against a

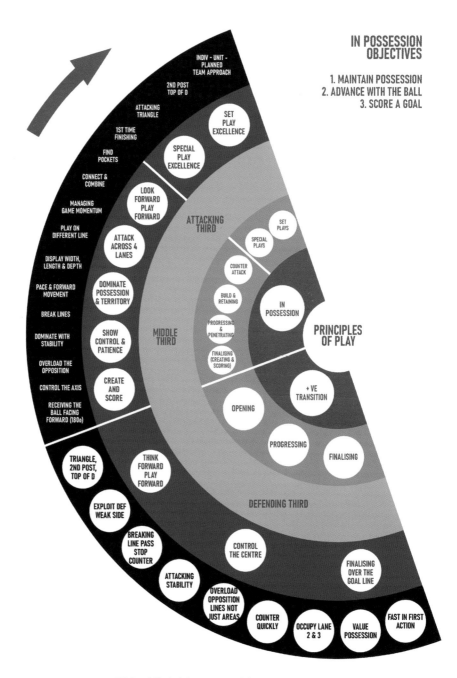

Michael Skubala's game model.

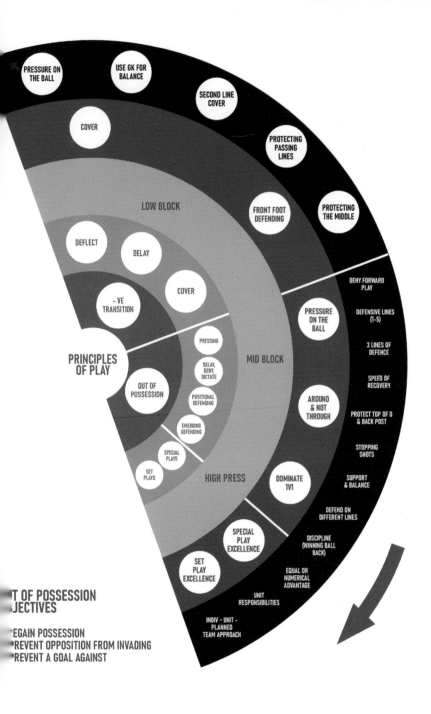

PRESSURE ON THE BALL

USE GK FOR BALANCE

SECOND LINE COVER

COVER

PROTECTING PASSING LINES

LOW BLOCK

FRONT FOOT DEFENDING

PROTECTING THE MIDDLE

DEFLECT

DELAY

DENY FORWARD PLAY

- VE TRANSITION

COVER

PRESSURE ON THE BALL

DEFENSIVE LINES (1-5)

3 LINES OF DEFENCE

PRINCIPLES OF PLAY

PRESSING

DELAY, DENY, DICTATE

MID BLOCK

SPEED OF RECOVERY

OUT OF POSSESSION

POSITIONAL DEFENDING

AROUND & NOT THROUGH

PROTECT TOP OF D & BACK POST

EMERGING DEFENDING

STOPPING SHOTS

SPECIAL PLAYS

SUPPORT & BALANCE

SET PLAYS

HIGH PRESS

DOMINATE 1V1

DEFEND ON DIFFERENT LINES

SPECIAL PLAY EXCELLENCE

DISCIPLINE (WINNING BALL BACK)

SET PLAY EXCELLENCE

EQUAL OR NUMERICAL ADVANTAGE

UNIT RESPONSIBILITIES

INDIV - UNIT - PLANNED TEAM APPROACH

T OF POSSESSION
JECTIVES

EGAIN POSSESSION
REVENT OPPOSITION FROM INVADING
REVENT A GOAL AGAINST

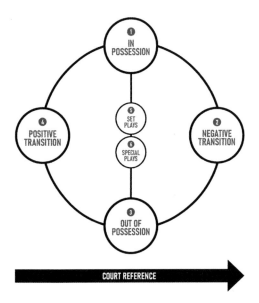

The moments of the game covered in the following pages.

team with a keeper comfortable with the ball at their feet, special plays are likely to be more common.

Each one of these moments is critical for either scoring or preventing a goal.

DEFINE THE COURT

Splitting the court into smaller sections enhances coaching points and allows players to understand high-level concepts more easily. There are a number of different ways that this can be done.

When teaching 'how we play', it is logical to split the court into thirds: the defending third (also known as the pressure zone), middle third (the progression zone) and the attacking third (the penetration zone). These invisible lines help players to understand concepts such as when to set up, when to press, how to move and why to execute certain strategies.

Similarly, splitting the court into four lanes can be a handy visual aid (some coaches split the court into three lanes, made up of two

team that likes to dominate possession, you are likely to be in positive transition and out of possession for much of the game. Against a

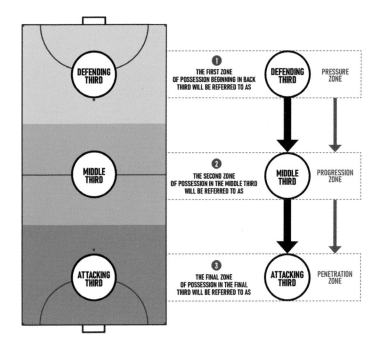

Splitting the court into three zones helps players understand what you want from them within sessions and matches.

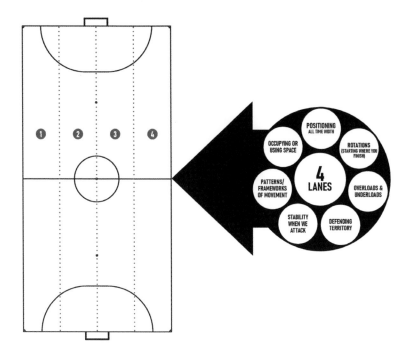

Using four lanes within a futsal court helps your players to understand complex principles.

outer lanes and one 10m central lane, while football coaches tend to split the pitch into five lanes).

Controlling the centre of the court or the axis is of incredible importance in futsal. Generally, the team that controls the centre of the court is the team that wins the game – as it is in all invasion games. To aid this understanding in players, the centre of the court can be split into two lanes: 2 and 3. This is to offset the balance of the opponents by playing slightly off centre when in possession. This forces the opponents to move their defensive structure to one side. If three of their four players are in lanes 1 and 2, it can give space to a spare attacker to go one-on-one in lane 4, for example.

These lanes also help players understand where to set up in an attack and why. It is particularly helpful when teaching players rotations – both in play and from restarts such as goalkeeper throws – and patterns of movement, allowing them to understand how to occupy and use space.

If players are in the same lane vertically, they should also refer to the lines that split the court into zones horizontally. As players improve their level of futsal, these visuals can help to empower them. Rather than telling the players what to do, coaches can ask them why they are in certain areas, how they are affecting the opposition and what their next movement should be. This detail sits behind a coach's game model and should become second nature to the players. To achieve this effect, the coach must make the game as simple as possible to understand for their players. Making the complex simple is an incredibly powerful tool in the coaching locker and should not be underestimated. The best coaches understand this well.

Ultimately, these two coaching aids help players to understand where to go and why. The four lanes, combined with the thirds, clearly show players how to offer stability when attacking by opening passing lines, providing cover and moving the opposition. Out of possession, they can be used to show defensive territory.

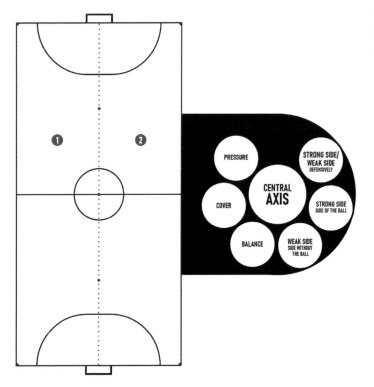

The futsal court's central axis alongside core principles to ensure superiority.

To bring out these concepts even more, the court can be simplified by splitting it down the middle to emphasize the central axis.

This division particularly helps to bring out strong and weak defensive sides. On an individual level, for example, left-footed players could be strongest on the right side of the court while right-footed players could be strongest on the left. This is so their dominant foot faces the majority of the court at all times, opening up more passing lines and easily enabling them to move with confidence toward the centre of the court.

On a team level, understanding strong and weak sides of the court helps to see where to attack a team, and also how to defend against an opponent. The central line down the court acts as a frame of reference for applying pressure on the ball, balancing attacks and giving cover to teammates, for example, if the attacking team is travelling down one line then the

defending team should all be in that half of the pitch.

Finally, when pressing opponents defensively, the court can be divided not just into thirds, but also into fifths.

These five lines can be defined as:

- 1 and 2: Pressing
- 2 and 3: Mid block
- 3 and 4: Low block
- 5: Special block

Beyond that, the goalkeeper is the ultimate line of defence.

Teams need to have multiple lines of defence to make it harder for an opponent to break them down. With England and in other club coaching, it was always preferable to have at least three lines of defence – plus the ultimate line of defence: the goalkeeper. This is so that defenders can provide support and cover if the

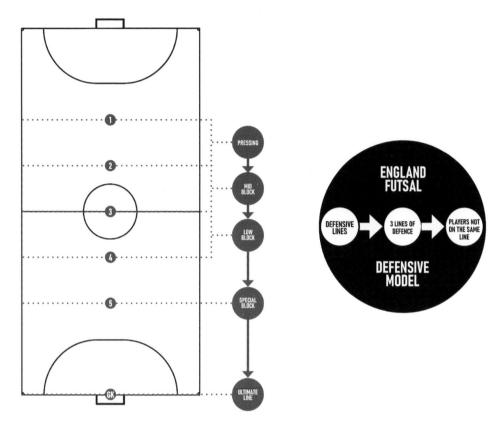

The five defensive lines. The type of block refers to where the highest player starts.

first line of defence is beaten but also coverage horizontally. The three lines of defence then use the five defensive lines on court as reference points for how high to press or how deep to set up. If the first line sets up on line 1 or 2, for example, the second and third lines take that as their cue for how deep to position themselves.

Though the five lines illustrate a defensive set-up, it is also helpful to show attacking concepts. By seeing which lines defenders are occupying, it is easier to work out how to disrupt those lines (ideally by making the court as big as possible).

Keeping these diagrams in mind, in addition to your coaching DNA and game model, will be important in the upcoming chapters. We're about to take a deep dive into futsal, centring on the moments of the game and principles of play that will help you coach to success regardless of whether you are a grassroots or elite coach in futsal or football. Remember, futsal is a game of space and time, and how you exploit them.

We're about to learn the best ways.

2 IN POSSESSION

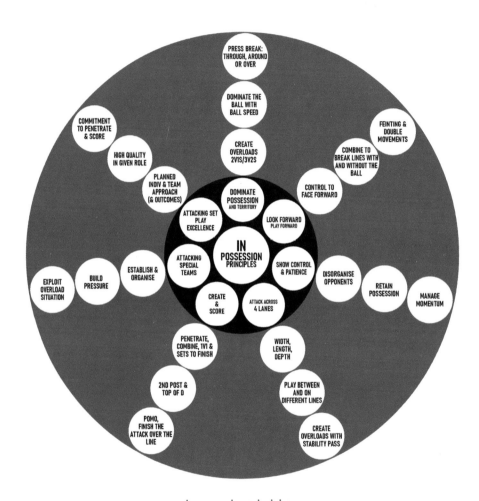

In possession principles.

In possession there is one ultimate aim: to score a goal. What excites players and coaches alike is that there are an incredible number of ways to do so.

By preparing your players for a range of eventualities, they increase their chances of success. To help you do so, in possession can be broken down into four distinct phases:

• Counter-attack/breaking pressure (often takes place in the defensive third)

Driving forward.

- Building and retaining (usually in the defensive or middle thirds)
- Progressing and penetrating (middle third)
- Creating and finalizing (attacking third)

These phases tend to occur in different areas of the court (except for a counter-attack, which can happen anywhere on the court).

To help guarantee success in each phase, there are seven core in possession principles, as shown in the game model in Chapter 1. They are:

- Dominate possession and territory
- Run forward, look forward, play forward

- Show control and patience
- Attack across four lanes
- Create and score
- Attacking special teams (to be detailed in Chapter 5)
- Attacking set-play excellence (to be detailed in Chapter 6)

The court is split into thirds, as well as four different attacking lanes. This helps to illustrate where a certain principle should take place. This is not to say, for example, that 1v1 excellence should only occur on the wings. Players should feel comfortable going 1v1 at

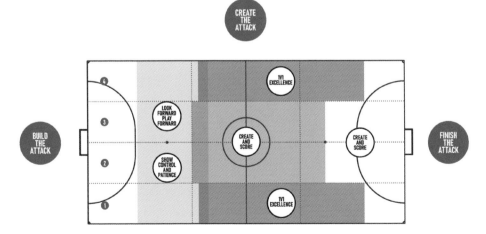

In possession principles, illustrated within the court to show where they are best used.

appropriate times. However, the wings are the ideal position on court to isolate opponents. They also provide security: if the attacker loses possession then the ball becomes more likely to bounce out for a restart from the sideline and it is less likely they will concede a counter-attack.

ROTATIONS

There are a variety of offensive set-ups to help bring out these principles within each phase. These set-ups encourage movement between players through rotation. If players stand still they are easy to mark. If they move, however, it creates uncertainty in a defence. The defender needs to make a number of calculations: do they follow and leave the space they are protecting? Do they exchange, commanding a teammate to instead mark the attacker? Do they simply stay in their space and allow the attacker to receive the ball? The more decisions a defender has to make, the more likely they are to get one wrong. It is these mistakes that the in possession team must use to their advantage.

Move on Up

When considering movement, at first look at the individual action. Then tie this in with the paired action, the triangle or threes action, and finally the full team action.

The best teams are fluid within the offensive set-ups. They decide which set-up to go with based on the skills and attributes of the players available, the opponents' weaknesses (*not* their strengths) and the game situation. The set-up will prove a starting point, with players moving into spaces based on a variety of factors, rather than simply rotating robotically.

At the elite level, the idea of set rotations is less relevant with teams preferring to adopt an in possession team identity which allows the players freedom in their movement and within a framework. This involves the team recognizing set moves with players reacting accordingly. To allow for such variety, however, the basics of rotations need to be engrained at individual, paired, and threes level. This will allow freedom within a framework.

Indeed, while rotations are important, the basis of understanding 1v1s and 2v2s within the rotations, along with the concepts underpinning them, is more important for your players. For example, when you rotate into the middle to receive a pass then look for a helping pass or wall pass, this is a 2v2 concept from the futsal threshold pyramid that allows for success within your framework.

The more dynamic 3-1 and 4-0 systems are most popular amongst elite futsal teams. Indeed, they have proven so effective that they are even being used in football. Teams such as Spain and Manchester City use similar rotations and movement patterns to utilize space and create overloads on the bigger pitch when adopting a positional style of play. Examples include the false 9, inverted full-backs and inverted wingers. This is where futsal is more unique than other small-sided games (such as five-a-side or seven-a-side) as the concepts for individuals and small groups are very similar to football due to the tactical element.

Fluid Systems

Futsal shouldn't just be one tactical system. At the top level, teams change between systems depending on the defensive actions or strategic intentions.

Basic Futsal playing systems/formations

Set-Up	What Is It?	Advantages	Disadvantages
1-2-2 (box)	Two players set up in the same horizontal line, with one set of two further forward in a different third. The two players tend to stick to their positions.	Less rotation makes it easier for novices to pick up. Players remain on their 'strong' sides. Natural playing width. Easy to understand for new players.	Less defensive cover if in negative transition (just two lines of defence). Fewer passing lines open. Easier for a defending team to shut off passing options and win the ball back.
1-3-1 (fixed pivot)	One fix and two wingers set up in the same horizontal line, with one pivot offering a forward pass. This forward is fixed, meaning they do not join the rotations and allow the three behind them to build possession before penetrating with a forward pass.	Increases the number of attacking passing lines. Chances to dominate the centre of the court through rotation. One side can be overloaded by the pivot. Provides total width to the team. Offers greater defensive security.	Needs a forward player (pivot or number 9) for it to work at its best. Attackers and pivot distances can become too long. Pivot can take the space others need to exploit. Limits space in behind all the defending team's lines.
1-3-1 (false pivot)	One fix and two wingers set up in the same horizontal line, with one pivot offering a forward pass. This forward is 'false', meaning that the position is interchangeable. As one of the three players rotates centrally or forward, the false pivot comes back into the play, receiving the ball deeper than they would as a fixed pivot.	Teams can exploit high and wide attacking areas. Useful for securing territory higher up the court. Exploit 1v1 and 2v2 situation on the open court side.	Harder to play than with a fixed forward player. Requires a different type of forward/pivot. Requires more team cohesion than a fixed pivot/forward.
4-0	Four players all play in the same third of the court in an attempt to create space behind an opponent that presses, or in between and around a zonal defence. Though all four players share a third, players typically operate in two sets of two, each set occupying a different vertical zone of the court. The ball moves laterally as players seek to penetrate with a forward pass. It very much looks like a back four playing out from the goalkeeper in football, with the centre halves dropping into the 18yd box to support.	Either flattens the opponent's defensive line or creates an overload. Disorganises and imbalances the opponent's defensive structure. Provides constant support to the ball. Increases the number of passing lines in order to exploit space in behind – ideal when an opponent is pressing.	Generally requires technically good players. Has limited cover and balance in defence if you lose the ball.

PRINCIPLES OF IN POSSESSION PLAY IN THE DEFENSIVE THIRD

Run Forward, Look Forward, Play Forward

In futsal, it's safer to play forward than it is to play sideways. If you lose possession when playing forward then at least one player can counter press: you! Playing forward should therefore always be the first thought of each player – not only because it's less risky, but also because it advances possession and moves the ball into an area where a goal is more likely to be scored (if intercepted, a sideways pass is far easier to counter-attack and the player who passed the ball is typically out of the game).

To play forward effectively, a player should have built a picture of the game long before receiving the ball (also developing their perception). They should already know the best passes to play, how many touches to use, whether to shoot or dribble and where their next move will likely be. When receiving the ball, they should do so facing forwards. This opens play 180 degrees and allows the player in possession to see as much of the court as possible. Their body shape should always reflect this. If the player receives the ball facing their own goal they are unlikely to be able to play a forward pass with a first time touch, for example, and if they do it is unlikely they will have built an accurate picture of the court. If they receive the ball side-on, it similarly limits passing options and means a player is more likely to have to be reactive to what happens in front of them rather than proactive. Furthermore, it makes them easier to press and acts as a trigger for defenders.

Ball speed is important in allowing forward play. The quicker the ball moves, the quicker the opponent must move. Quick, firm passes therefore open up more gaps in an opponent's defence and help to create opportunities to

The first thought of every futsal player: can I play forward?

exploit space. The pass into the player should be firm and along the floor, allowing them to either play first time or take a positive touch to set up the next play. If the player elects to pass, this too should be with the appropriate ball speed. If the pass is entering the final third, its quality is magnified still further. There are, however, times when slower passes may be optimal. These can entice an opponent into an area, which may then create space in behind when they are lured into pressing the ball. If teammates are blocking for passes, slowing play can entice opponents into attempting to break past the blocks, creating space in the area they've immediately vacated. Staying on the ball can therefore create overloads.

Staying on the Ball

Staying on the ball to draw in pressure from the opponent as an individual or collective line can create space and time behind them to attack. Players must understand 'why' they are staying on the ball.

Playing forward disrupts the opposition's defensive lines. Complemented with effective and forward movement into attacking space, it

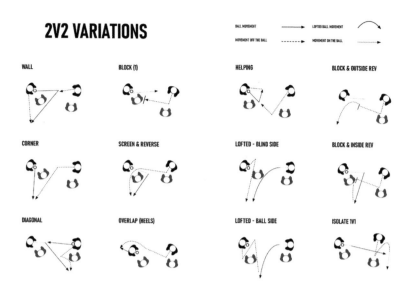

2V2 VARIATIONS

There are numerous solutions to creating space and penetrating lines in 2v2 situations.

is likely to cause disorganisation in the defence, as well as overloads. These offensive overloads can further be brought out by combinations and connections in between lines, usually working in pairs or threes (as mentioned in the futsal threshold concept pyramid). Such movements include **parallel passes** or corner runs (passing along a vertical lane), **wall passes** (a one-two bounced between players, usually around an opponent), **helping passes** (a forward pass followed by a set back to the passer who has continued their forward run along the line of the ball), overlaps or underlapping runs, **heels** (rolling the ball slightly behind your body for a teammate to run onto) or **blocks** on an opponent (either direct blocks to create space for a player in possession or indirect blocks to open up passing lines).

These movements are not limited to futsal. They are commonplace in all forms of football,

from 3v3 right up to the eleven-a-side game. These small battles take place all across the pitch and the court.

Liar, Liar!

Futsal is a game for liars in possession. By disguising movements, disguising passes and blocking opponents, such lies can increase the ease of playing forward for their teammates.

SESSION PLANS

The following sessions are designed to work on looking forward to play forward. Key coaching points are detailed, along with extra information to help you get the most out of each session.

ICE HOCKEY

FOCUS: Run Forward, Look Forward, Play Forward

ORGANISATION

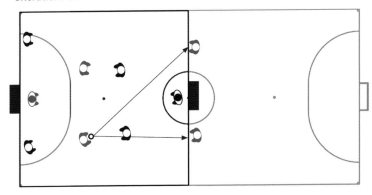

PROGRESSION

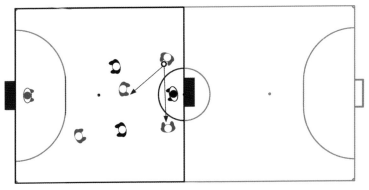

Number of Players: 10 (8+2 goalkeepers)

Equipment: 2× goals, balls, bibs

IP Objectives: To develop and acquire principles of facing forward and playing forward, including using combinations and connections as a two and in sets of three players.

OOP Objectives: To develop principles of defending as an individual with core skills and laterality. Also stopping forward passes and protecting the middle.

ORGANISATION

Create a 15×20m area with two goals. Players will play 2v2 in the middle. Each team has a further two players who act as pivots, standing either side of the goal they are attacking. To score a goal, the players in the middle must pass the ball to the pivots before they can score. It is the pivot's job to set the ball back to the players to finish. These pivots cannot be tackled. When the ball turns over, the opposition has to do the same. To start the practice, goalkeepers take the ball in their hands and roll it to a teammate. At first, the ball has to go to a player in the middle and not straight into the pivot from the keeper.

PROGRESSIONS

- Limit the players in the middle to two touches and the pivots to one touch
- Change the length of the games so that two goals wins and winners stay on
- Pivots can play direct to the other pivot on the second post (one-touch-finish only)
- Pivots can finish at the back post direct from passes forward from the middle
- When the middle players are tired they can run and change with the pivots by high-fiving them. Pivots cannot enter the court until the high-five has happened

COACHING POINTS

Before Phase –
- The first movement is always down to the 1v1 skills of earning the back of your opposite player or checking to get space. This creates confusion in an opponent, who must turn to check where the player is

During Phase –
- Look forward to play forward
- Ensure high quality of forward pass
- Quality of set from pivots
- Disguise passes – futsal is a game for liars and cheats, making players hard to read

After Phase –
- Movement to get the ball back
- Use double movements to create space again: the first movement is usually forward and always done for the opposition defender; the second is then to attack the space created from that first movement
- Move to clear the space for the other teammate to come around

LINKS TO FOOTBALL
Across the football pitch, players work in pairs to play forward and create space. In midfield, for example, a number 8 and 10 will combine and move alongside the number 9, playing as a 2 or 3 with vertical movements.

PENDULUM PIVOT

FOCUS: Look Forward, Play Forward

ORGANISATION

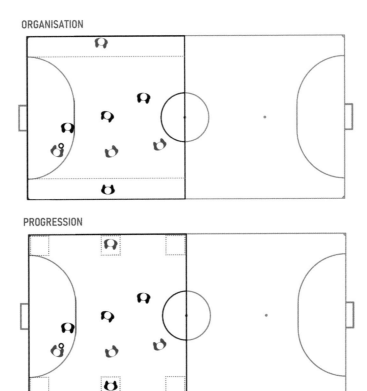

PROGRESSION

Number of Players: 8

Equipment: Bibs, balls, cones

IP Objectives: Players look to run forward, face forward and play forward into a pivot.

OOP Objectives: Press individuals and passing lines in order to stop forward passes and win the ball back.

ORGANISATION
In a half court or 20×20m area, two teams play in a directional 3v3. The teams attempt to get the ball into their pivot player, who is standing at the end they are attacking in one of three marked boxes (measuring 1×1m). These are safe zones that defenders cannot enter. Passes into the pivot's safe zone must be played under head height to start with. Once the ball goes into a pivot, the attacking team receives the ball once more and changes their direction of attack, now aiming to play to the opposite pivot. The defending team must change their pivot at the same time as the attacking team does.

PROGRESSIONS
• Can play over head height

- Must play with two touches
- Each team can play with two pivots to make it easier
- The pivot can only receive in one box

COACHING POINTS
Before Phase –
- Moulding and creating space to face forward on the ball (fake movements, checks, body positioning)
- Combining as a two to play forward
- Supporting or attacking as a third player to play around or penetrate

During Phase –
- Combination play with two and three players
- Quality of forward pass to pivot
- Receiving skills of pivot – protect the ball with your body

- Use the width of the court – emphasize the four lanes

After Phase –
- Negative transition to defend the ball
- Supporting the combination pass
- Gain height, width and depth when the game pendulums the other way in possession, switching play quickly and efficiently

LINKS TO FOOTBALL
This game helps midfield players who are learning to connect with a number 9 or number 10. It also works on three forward players learning the responsibility of pressing as a front two or three to stop forward passing, then transitioning quickly when they win the ball back.

DEVELOPING VERTICAL 2V2S

FOCUS: Look Forward, Play Forward

ORGANISATION

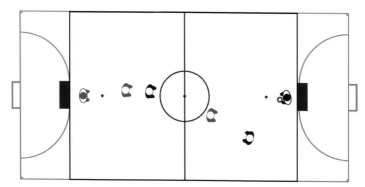

Number of Players: 4+ (with 2 goalkeepers)

Equipment: Bibs, balls, goals

IP Objectives: Players use feints off the ball to receive in space and play forwards, then combine with a pivot.

OOP Objectives: Stop forward play, then track and defend forward runs if unsuccessful.

ORGANISATION

With a goal at the edge of either 6m area, a court of 28×20m is created. This court then has a halfway line added, which makes for two zones. Players are put into teams of two. One player must occupy the defensive half while the other must go in the attacking half and act as a pivot.

The goalkeeper starts the game by either throwing the ball directly to the pivot in the attacking half or playing it short to the player in the defensive half. This player must then play to the pivot.

Once the ball is controlled by the pivot, the support player in the defensive half can choose to either join in by running into the attacking half or allow the pivot to play in a 1v1. If they do join in, then the second defender can follow them. If the pivot loses the ball and the defender wins it, they can immediately play to their pivot for a 1v1 or 2v1.

PROGRESSIONS
- Defenders cannot track runners, leaving 2v1s
- The second defender can track back no matter what the support attacker does

COACHING POINTS
Before Phase –
- Movement to receive the ball is key here
- Can players use double movements to gain possession and face forward to play forward?

During Phase –
- Quality forward passes that allow for instant attacking play
- Forward runs to combine with the pivot (attack the space)
- Protecting and staying on the ball as a pivot with a view to turning or setting to create scoring opportunities

After Phase –
- Counter pressing the defender to stop transition
- Recovery runs to defend

LINKS TO FOOTBALL
In this practice you could swap the goalkeeper for a midfielder who has to play a forward pass for the second midfielder to run off. It is fantastic for teaching attacking players how to connect with those ahead of them on the pitch, using depth to create scoring opportunities.

THROUGH THE THIRDS – GRAEME DELL

FOCUS: Playing Forward as a Priority

Graeme Dell was England's first ever futsal manager and spent five years in charge, including for England's first ever UEFA Futsal Championship. He is the youngest coach to ever receive the full FA Coaching Licence. He is now a FIFA Coaching Instructor, working as an ambassador for the game of futsal.

ORGANISATION

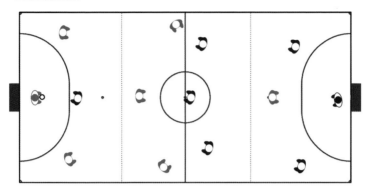

Number of Players: Up to 16 (but never more than 5v5 in any third to keep the game realistic)

Equipment: Bibs, balls, cones

IP Objectives: Play through the thirds as quickly as possible.

OOP Objectives: Recover the ball as quickly as possible.

ORGANISATION

A full court is split evenly into thirds with players occupying each third. To start, players cannot leave their thirds. The game begins when the red team's goalkeeper rolls the ball out to a teammate in the defensive third. The reds then attempt to pass into the middle third. Once this is done, they then pass into the final third where they can score. The player that passes the ball is allowed to join the attacking player to make it a 2v2 in the final third.

Once the action is over, the blues begin from their goalkeeper.

PROGRESSIONS

- One of the reds in the middle third can drop in to make it a 3v1 in the building phase

- If one of the reds drops in then one of the blues can follow to make it a 3v2
- One player can be released from each third
- Goals can be scored from anywhere
- Transitions can be completely open with no restrictions
- Work the session as an underloaded activity – when players are competent enough

COACHING POINTS

Before Phase –
- Movement to create forward passing
- Facing forward to play forwards with quality

During Phase –
- Passing forwards with quality
- Short, quick passes through the thirds
- Try to play a pass so the next one can be played forwards

After Phase –
- Follow your pass to support the ball – play and follow
- Try to be in a position to play forward again
- Run forwards before moving backwards to create individual space

LINKS TO FOOTBALL

With the growth of short kicks from the goalkeeper, an increasing number of football teams are opting to play through the thirds. They invite pressure to then exploit the space in behind. When the ball progresses into midfield, the forward pass and following movement is particularly relevant so that teams can break lines. The transition element also provides instant feedback for quality of pass – essential for playing through the thirds in either football or futsal.

THROUGH THE TUNNELS – MIGUEL RODRIGO

FOCUS: Combining in 2v1s

Miguel Rodrigo is a Spanish coach who spent seven years in charge of the Japanese national futsal team. Such was his impact that the Japanese media dubbed him 'The Magician'. He won two Asian Futsal Championships with Japan. Now a UEFA Technical Observer and FIFA Futsal Instructor, he has also coached in Spain, Italy, Russia, Thailand and Vietnam. Here he shares a session on 2v1 excellence to progress through the court.

ORGANISATION

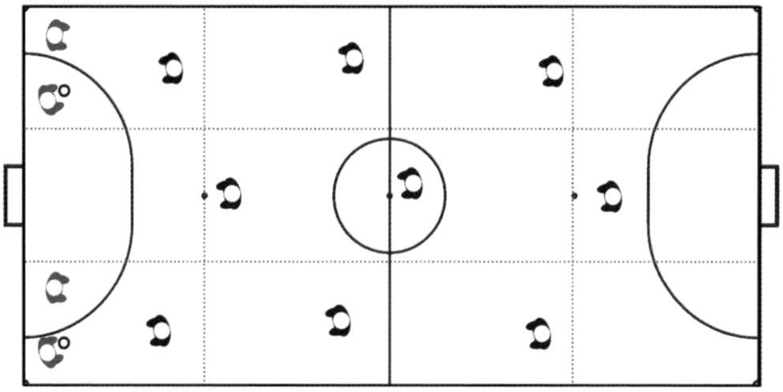

PROGRESSION

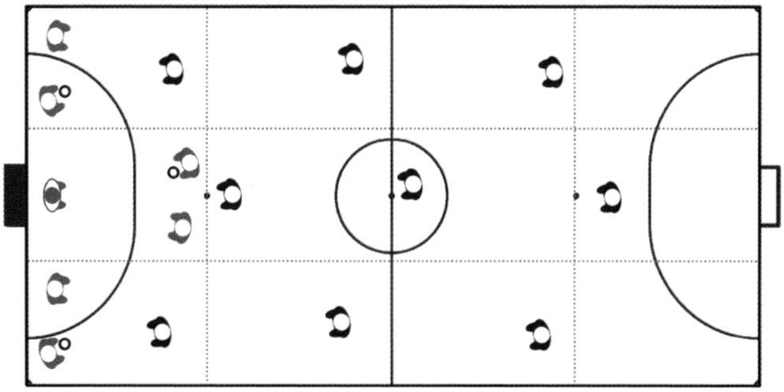

Number of Players: 13

Equipment: Bibs, balls, cones, goals

IP Objectives: Advance possession using the overload.

OOP Objectives: Develop 1v1 defending skills when underloaded.

ORGANISATION

The court is split into three channels of around 6m width. There are then four zones of equal length across the court. A defender occupies each of the highest three zones.

In pairs, attackers attempt to make their way through each zone. They aim to dribble past the first defender and enter the next zone, where they face the following defender. Once they get to the end of the first channel, they turn and make their way through the middle channel, once again attempting to beat all the defenders in the zones. If the attackers manage to beat all nine defenders then they have completed the tunnel.

If any of the defenders manage to win the ball back from the attackers, they switch places with the attacker who lost possession.

PROGRESSIONS

- Play with a goalkeeper at one end: players must then score in that zone to progress to the next one (there's also an option to add goalkeepers at each end)

COACHING POINTS

Before Phase –

- Support depending on the pressure on the ball

- Speed of approach (slow to entice, quick to move past)

During Phase –

- Different types of horizontal and vertical runs to combine to play forward and take advantage of the overload
- Blocks to allow for the dribble
- Engage the defender
- Change of speed and direction to escape the defender
- Body orientation for all players (can the defender force the attackers in one direction, using the line as an extra defender?)

After Phase –

- Movement to support the ball carrier again
- Travel centrally with the ball to keep options open
- Spatial awareness to see where is best to attack next
- Assess where the next defender is and how fast they are approaching

LINKS TO FOOTBALL

All players need to be comfortable on the ball. With progressive ball carries becoming a key piece of data, players will increasingly become encouraged to run forward with the ball. Doing so helps to break lines of defence and disorganises opponents. Most importantly, however, this is a fun game that can make for a great warm-up.

DOMINATE POSSESSION AND TERRITORY

You cannot score a goal without possession of the ball. Dominating the ball and dominating areas of the court both increase the chances of scoring a goal. There are three main ways to dominate both:

1. Create **overloads** on the first defensive line that influences the opponent's second line. This relates to the combinations discussed in the look forward, play forward section. These overloads should occur in 1v1, 2v2 and 3v3 scenarios.

The Jewel in the Crown

Overloads happen in a flash in futsal. Finding the overload, then exploiting the advantage, is what separates the best teams from the rest.

2. Dominate the ball with court position and **high ball speed**. Players should ideally receive the ball facing forward if possible so that they can control the 1v1 situation and dominate their opponent, with the option to have at least two routes out of the pressure. To keep ball speed high, touches should be limited in areas of high pressure. The fewer touches that players take on the ball, the quicker it will move around the court to disrupt opponents.

3. **Attack space** through, around and beyond with quality forward passes and disguised movement.

Control Space by Creating Space

Increase the likelihood of success of double movements by encouraging players to turn their hips and shoulders in one direction. This is more likely to fool the defender than merely stepping in one direction to then fake the movement.

SESSION PLANS

The following sessions are designed to work on dominating possession and territory. Key coaching points are detailed, along with extra information to help you get the most out of each session.

On the attack.

COMBO TO BUILD

FOCUS: Creating Overloads to Build Play

ORGANISATION

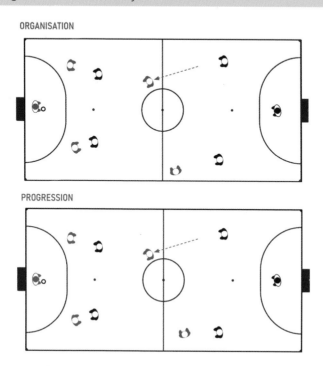

PROGRESSION

Number of Players: 10 (8+2 goalkeepers)

Equipment: 2× goals, balls, bibs

IP Objectives: To understand how to support and create a 3v2 when building out of pressure, progressing into how to use a 3v2 when finishing.

OOP Objectives: To develop principles of defending as an individual and when outnumbered by closing the middle and forcing opponents around rather than through.

ORGANISATION

On a full court, two teams face off against each other. Each has one goalkeeper and four outfield players. Two outfield players must remain in the defensive half at all times when defending, while the other two outfield players must remain in the attacking half when defending. Nobody can cross the halfway line when they are defending. However, the team in possession is allowed one outfield player that can drop into either half to create a 3v2 overload. This allows an overload for when a team is building possession or finishing on goal.

PROGRESSIONS
* The player switching halves can only go in for four seconds
* The player switching halves can only have two touches
* The player switching halves can only have one touch

- The player switching halves cannot go back to their original half; instead it must be another player on their team

COACHING POINTS

Before Phase –

- Focus on when, where and how players should support to create overloads
- Look at the body shape of the offensive players. Can they face forward when receiving to help them play out of pressure?

During Phase –

- Quality and selection of passing combinations (wall pass, helping pass or parallel pass)
- Play passes that break the lines
- Use the width of the court – emphasize the four lanes

After Phase –

- Movement to support the next phase of possession
- Movement to lose marker (ideally when their head turns to look at the ball)
- Creating width, depth and height where possible after the pass
- Playing in the most space to look forward and play forward

LINKS TO FOOTBALL

Centre backs who play out from the back need to create the space to play forward. Often they combine with the holding midfield player to break the first line of pressure coming from the forwards.

DEVELOPING 2V2S IN A SYSTEM

FOCUS: Paired Movement and Numerical Advantage

ORGANISATION

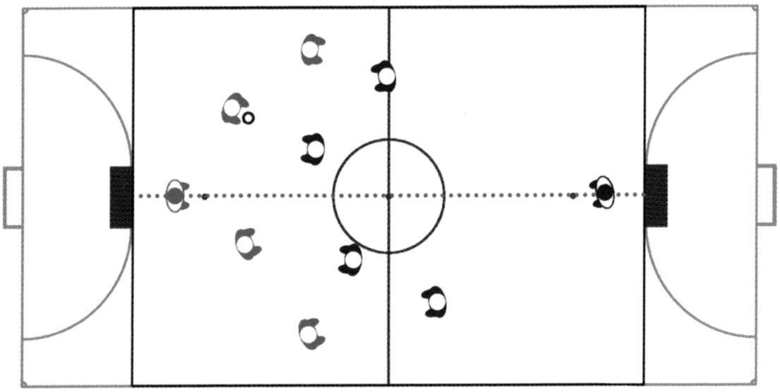

PROGRESSION

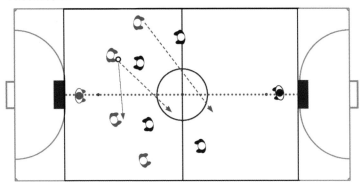

Number of Players: 10 (8+2 goalkeepers)

Equipment: 2× goals, balls, bibs, cones

IP Objectives: To understand how paired movements can unlock space and create forward opportunities.

OOP Objectives: Press, cover and balance in order to win the ball back and attack.

ORGANISATION
In a 28×20m area with two goals, players play a 4v4 with one goalkeeper each. The court is split down the central axis to create a 2v2 in each half. Players cannot cross this central axis. Instead, they can combine with their teammate in their own half or on the two players on the opposite side through passing and intelligent movement such as blocks and screens. Kick-ins and corners can be played as usual with other standard rules applying.

PROGRESSIONS
- The attacker who plays the ball into the opposite half can join for that play without being followed by an opponent to create an overload
- The attacker who doesn't play the ball into the opposite half can follow in on a pass into that area

COACHING POINTS
Before Phase –
- Timing of movement to receive the ball
- Can players position themselves with width or depth to maximize space?
- Double movements (one to shift the defender, one to exploit the space)
- Blocks and screens
- Support the 2v2 on the opposite side

During Phase –
- Work with the different possibilities of paired movements
- Can players use horizontal and vertical movement?

After Phase –
- Get into position again quickly to receive and play an attacking pass
- Can players provide an option for their teammates?

LINKS TO FOOTBALL
Vertical and horizontal combinations happen all over the football pitch, particularly in the final third and wide areas. This practice also develops third player runs once progressed, alongside how to make the most of the over-load once that third player run happens. This mimics a midfielder bursting forward to support the attack.

BOX JUMPING

FOCUS: Creating Overloads to Build Play

ORGANISATION

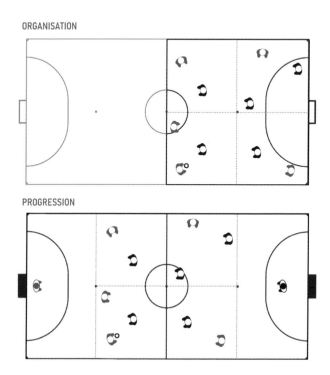

PROGRESSION

Number of Players: 10

Equipment: 2× goals, balls, bibs

IP Objectives: Vision before receiving the ball and awareness of pictures around the player, allowing them to play effectively. Players should also occupy and create space for others to use.

OOP Objectives; The game will create 2v2, 2v1, 1v2 and 1v1 situations, allowing defenders to press and block passing lines – or jump out of boxes if they have two players in one box. Defenders need to work together as a unit rather than having just one player chasing.

ORGANISATION
In a half court measuring anything from 15×15m to 20×20m, teams keep possession while playing 5v5. This area is then further split into four squares. Both teams must keep a player in each of the four squares during the exercise.

PROGRESSIONS
- Limit the amount of touches to two
- Attackers can move anywhere but defenders must fill a minimum of one box
- To win a point, the in possession team must pass into all four boxes in any given possession
- Put two small goals at each end. Once the in possession team has reached a set

number of passes or played into all four boxes they can break out to score

- Add two normal goals at each end with goalkeepers. Once a team has made a set amount of passes or got around all four boxes, they can break out in a 2v1 to score against a goalkeeper

COACHING POINTS
Before Phase –

- Players must create space in a 1v1 to be able to get on the ball – double movements are needed (move 1yd to gain 5yd, running past the defender's shoulder to force them to turn)
- Players can work together to move around boxes and create overloads against defenders
- Players need to know their next pass before receiving the ball. Scanning should therefore be encouraged to paint pictures of players' surroundings

During Phase –

- Take an oriented first touch out of pressure
- Quality of pass
- Encourage combination play, understanding when players have numerical supremacy

After Phase –

- Movement to get the ball back
- Make your box as big as possible with intelligent movement
- Connect with a teammate using horizontal and vertical movement

LINKS TO FOOTBALL
Players need to understand where and why they rotate all over the pitch, alongside principles of creating and moulding space. This exercise also works on quick switches of play and combination play in tight areas.

THE MATADOR – PAUL MCGUINNESS

FOCUS: Combination Play within the Flow of the Game

Paul McGuinness spent twenty-eight years as a player and coach at the Manchester United academy and is now the Head of Academy Player Development at Leicester City. He also worked as a National Coach Developer and U16 National Coach for the Football Association.

ORGANISATION

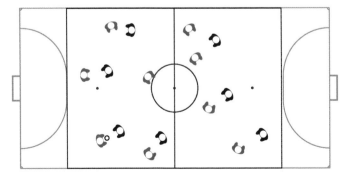

Number of Players: Any. The one essential is that the area is tight. In this instance we have gone for a 10v7 in a 32x20m area.

Equipment: Balls, bibs, cones

IP Objectives: To play through and combine with teammates travelling from one side to the other, learning to read the flow in the game.

OOP Objectives: Win the ball back and transition immediately by dribbling.

ORGANISATION

Two teams play in a tight area. The attacking team has an overload. It is their task to work the ball from one end line and back to score a goal. End lines are used rather than goals to keep the flow and momentum of the game going.

Individuals on the attacking team should attempt to score without using single passes. Instead, they should look to play to a teammate and receive the ball back, ideally through the middle of the court rather than the outside. For success, players need to explore getting close to opponents when in possession without getting caught (getting close to the fire without getting burnt). This engages the defender, entices them in, and therefore makes it easier to exploit the space behind – as well as gain an advantage on them in the next phase of play.

If the defending team wins the ball they have to either dribble to the side of the pitch or an end line to score a goal. The attacking team should counter press immediately to stop this from happening.

PROGRESSIONS
* Reduce the overload or even match up the numbers of the attacking and defensive teams

COACHING POINTS
Before Phase –
* Perception and scanning skill to see teammates and space
* Creating space to get on the ball
* Third player runs off the ball to combine are key

During Phase –
* Use disguise on the ball for passing and getting it back
* Use of body to find solutions out of pressure
* Intimidation by use of individual skill
* Leaving passes late to beat opponents but not getting caught (getting close to the opponent without getting burnt)

After Phase –
* Play and move constantly
* Change the speed and direction of movement to evade opponents
* Think about crossover and movements with two players vertically and horizontally
* Counter press after losing possession

LINKS TO FOOTBALL
Combination play is needed in every area of the pitch to advance possession – particularly if a team is being pressed. In this exercise players develop combination play, feeling the flow of the game and playing with purpose and direction.

THE STADIUM GAME – PETER STURGESS

FOCUS: Staying on the Ball through Individual Possession

FIFA Futsal Instructor, FA Lead for the Foundation Phase and former England Head Coach Peter Sturgess has contributed the following session to work on bravery on the ball and maintaining territory in possession. You can find more of Peter's sessions in his book *Futsal: Training, Technique and Tactics.*

ORGANISATION

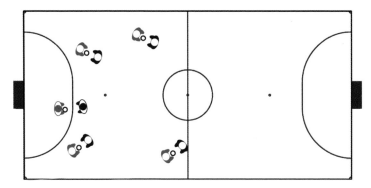

Number of Players: 6+

Equipment: 2× goals, balls, bibs

IP Objectives: Recognize space to stay on the ball as an individual.

OOP Objectives: Pressing 1v1 to win the ball back.

ORGANISATION

Players are split evenly into two teams and take part in a normal game on a normal pitch. When a goal is scored, the game is halted and players enter the 'stadium'. If the red team score, then the 'stadium' is the red team's half. Each red player is given a ball and paired with a blue opponent to play against in the stadium.

When the coach starts the stadium game, the red players are each attempting to keep their ball within the red stadium. The blue players are all trying to win the ball and take it back to their own stadium (the blue defensive half).

At the end of the allotted time the coach counts how many balls are in each stadium. If the reds have more balls in their stadium then the original goal stands. But if the blues have won more balls than the reds, the goal does not count and the original game continues at 0-0.

Once another goal has been scored, the stadium game restarts in the 'stadium' of the team that has just scored.

PROGRESSIONS

*   Alter the exercise to work on defending by giving the opposing team possession of the balls in the stadium game and making the team that has just scored win possession back to allow their goal to count

- Alter the numbers in the stadium game: it could be a 1v2, 2v2 or even 2v1

COACHING POINTS

Before Phase –

- Players must read the space they want to protect the ball in

During Phase –

- Change of speed and direction with the ball
- Protect the ball
- Skills and tricks to evade opponents
- Accelerations and decelerations with the ball

After Phase –

- Counter as quickly as possible to win the ball back

LINKS TO FOOTBALL

While there are huge physical returns in this game to aid conditioning, it also teaches bravery in possession and 1v1 skills. These are particularly important in a player-to-player defensive system where individual superiority is key.

HEXAGON RONDO – MIGUEL RODRIGO

FOCUS: Combining in Triangles

ORGANISATION

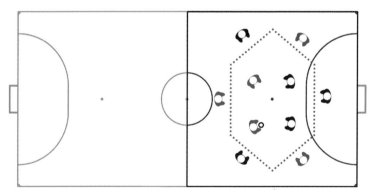

Number of Players: 10 with 1 goalkeeper

Equipment: Goal, balls, bibs, cones

IP Objectives: Support by offering a passing line that creates a triangle.

OOP Objectives: Pressing as a pair to win the ball back.

ORGANISATION

Taking part in one half of a full court, players are split into two teams of five. Two from each team then enter the hexagon, marked out in the centre of the playing area. The rest of the players set up on the outside of the hexagon with players alternating in position (two reds cannot set up next to each other).

Inside the hexagon, a simple 2v2 takes place. Players in the middle are allowed to combine with their teammates on the outside of the hexagon. The shape of the hexagon encourages plenty of triangle shapes. Players in the middle have an unlimited amount of touches with which to play while those on the outside have just one touch. Those on the outside cannot play a pass directly to anyone else on the outside.

PROGRESSIONS

- Once a team has made five passes they can break out of the hexagon and attempt to score against a goalkeeper
- Increase the size of the playing area and make it 3v3, though still taking place within a hexagon to encourage triangle play

COACHING POINTS

Before Phase –

- Movement in the middle to lose opponents

During Phase –

- Protect the ball
- Body shape to open up passing lines
- Blocks
- Combination play
- Changes of speed to draw in opponent

After Phase –

- Recognize the space to create another passing option after playing a pass

LINKS TO FOOTBALL

Triangles happen not only all over the futsal court, but also all over the football pitch. They allow for at least two passing options, helping players to make effective decisions and advance possession.

PRINCIPLES OF IN POSSESSION PLAY IN THE MIDDLE THIRD

Show Control and Patience

Futsal is a game of timing. And changing the pace is sometimes just as important as playing quickly. You cannot control possession or territory if your team is impatient and always rushing to move the ball forward. Players should always look to play forward, but if a suitable option is not on then they should wait, retaining possession until the moment arrives.

Having possession of the ball is effectively a chance to out-think your opponents. It gives the opportunity to dominate play by recognizing time, space, the position of the ball and the position of opponents in every moment. It is then effective decisions that help a team to outplay their opponents. If playing forward is possible then the ball needs to move forward with quality and be complemented by forward entry from the team. This movement off the ball is key to create space, occupy space and use space. It isn't just about outplaying an opponent; it is also about outworking them.

Showing control and patience is therefore about building a play steadily, retaining possession in the process while continuing to offer a threat. This is done by attacking space and playing with a focal point. The possession should be seen as a chance to disorganise the opponents and manage game momentum. If your team has the ball, the opposition cannot hurt you.

Defining Importance

In futsal the pivot generally refers to the most forward player, whereas in football it tends to refer to a midfielder. In invasion games the pivot is the position that the team is built around. In futsal it's therefore considered that play is built around the most forward player.

SESSION PLANS

The following sessions are designed to work on showing control and patience. Key coaching points are detailed, along with extra information to help you get the most out of each session.

Be brave on the ball.

TEAM BOXES

FOCUS: Team Cohesion in Possession

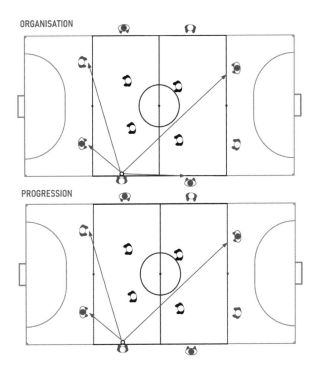

Number of Players: 12

Equipment: Balls, bibs (3 different colours)

IP Objectives: Keep the quality of pass to players high around the outside, developing into first line passes, second line passes and line-breaking passes to the pivot or most advanced player.

OOP Objectives: Work as a unit to get the ball back as quickly as possible.

ORGANISATION
Split players into three teams. Two of the teams stand alternated outside the area (ideally 10×10m) and attempt to keep possession amongst themselves (they can play to any player). The third team is in the middle of the area. They must chase the ball to win back possession. When the team in the middle wins the ball back they swap with the team that lost the ball. These swaps must be direct, so they stand in the same positions (maintaining the alternate colours on the outside).

PROGRESSIONS
- Players cannot play to the player on the same side of the court as them

- Two touches maximum on the outside
- Players can move up and down the sides
- Players can switch places on the outside to encourage rotations

COACHING POINTS
Before Phase –
- Players must face forward to play forward and not get trapped on the ball
- Players can move up and down the side to open passing lines
- See the next pass through the lines before the ball arrives

During Phase –
- Take an oriented first touch
- High quality of short and line-breaking passes through the middle

After Phase –
- Support again to offer another pass
- Support and move along the line to open passing lines

LINKS TO FOOTBALL
This exercise develops combination play and can be used as a warm-up with huge psychological returns such as working as a team.

THE 100 PASS GAME

FOCUS: Keeping Possession

ORGANISATION

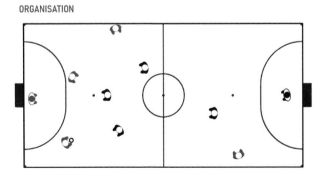

Number of Players: 10

Equipment: Balls, bibs (3 different colours)

IP Objectives: Recognize space: when to play short and when to play long over the press.

OOP Objectives: Work as a unit to half the pitch, condensing the space for the attackers to win the ball back as quickly as possible.

ORGANISATION

In a basic set-up, two teams play on a full court. The objective is not to score a goal but to make 100 passes. The team that does this first wins (the coach keeps count).

Teams are allowed to use either goalkeeper, who can only play with their feet (and cannot play directly to the other goalkeeper). Defenders should press aggressively to win the ball back. The game is multi-directional.

PROGRESSIONS
- Add a floater that the team must play through
- Add a defensive floater so the in possession team is underloaded
- Once a team hits twenty passes they can go and score in either goal (this can be developed further: if they score in the goal they

get a goal and to continue the count from twenty; if they miss they go back to zero)

COACHING POINTS
Before Phase –
- Body shape before receiving the ball
- Find the biggest spaces to play in

During Phase –
- Change of speed
- Change of direction
- Switch play horizontally and vertically
- Don't stop the ball dead – keep it moving
- Entice opponents in to exploit the space behind
- Use the horizontal and vertical lanes in the court to maximize space

After Phase –
- Support to get on the ball again to play out of pressure
- Transition

LINKS TO FOOTBALL
Players need to be comfortable keeping possession all over the pitch, embracing pressure from opponents and seeing it as a chance to exploit the space that the pressure leaves rather than worrying about losing the ball.

ATTACK ACROSS FOUR LANES

Using all four lanes in an attack allows a team to play with **width, length and depth** to make the court as big as possible. This provides more opportunities to penetrate by opening up space, and subsequently more passing lines (it is therefore important a team also **plays on different lines**, so that they can impact the first line of defence while influencing the second line). Occupying the wide lanes allows for rapid switching of play to disrupt a defence,

while the space created in the centre increases the possibilities to play forward and use attacking triangles. Importantly, using all four lanes gives stability to an attack.

By playing on different lines, it becomes possible to **find pockets of space** between defensive lines, which is where combination play can prove effective. This can be done both horizontally and vertically.

When attacking, teams should always look to **control and dominate the centre of the court** by attacking across the four lanes.

This opens up passing options forward, left and right, creating more indecision in a defending team. Players should decide exactly where to position themselves depending on the pressure of the ball, creating opportunities for forward passes using dynamic movements. At least one player should always provide cover when attacking to reduce the counter-attack threat and **provide stability** behind the ball.

Four Lanes

In some cultures coaches use three lanes of different sizes. It's important to note that whatever you decide to build as your model, you are consistent with your players.

SESSION PLANS

The following sessions are designed to work on attacking across four lanes. Key coaching points are detailed, along with extra information to help you get the most out of each session.

END ZONES

ORGANISATION

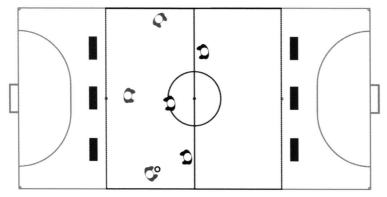

Number of Players: 6

Equipment: 6× mini goals, balls, bibs

IP Objectives: Combining as a three to score, using the full width of the court.

OOP Objectives: Defend as a unit to regain possession.

ORGANISATION

A court is marked out with end zones at each end. These contain three mini goals spaced evenly across the court. Inside the court, two teams play in a 3v3 game. To score, they must break into the end zone where they finish with one touch. Defenders are allowed into the end zones.

PROGRESSIONS
- Alter the number of players on court
- Use a goalkeeper to cover all three goals, allowing players to finish from anywhere (not just the end zone)
- Limit players to no more than three touches

COACHING POINTS
Before Phase –
- Ability to lose your opponent
- Create space to play forward, either travelling with the ball or from forward attacking passes

During Phase –
- 1v1 skills to dribble or travel with the ball (emphasize this in lanes 1 and 4 when opponents are isolated)

- Combine with teammates using paired movements (wall pass, overlaps, corner/parallel runs) or diagonal passes
- Emphasize the use of all four lanes with isolation of opponents happening primarily in lanes 1 and 4

After Phase –
- Support teammates, either with a safe option or an attacking movement to receive higher depending on the defensive pressure

LINKS TO FOOTBALL
This exercise develops combination play and can be used as a warm-up with huge social returns, such as working as a team, and psychological returns such as when to make horizontal or vertical runs based on the actions of teammates and opponents. The three goals mimic a midfield three attempting to play into a front three, or a front three playing defence-splitting passes and then running on to through balls to finish.

UNDER AND OVER

FOCUS: Attacking with Overloads, Using the Width of the Court

ORGANISATION

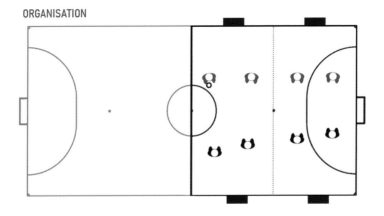

Number of Players: 8

Equipment: 4× mini goals, balls, bibs

IP Objectives: Switch play to create overloads as a 3v2.

OOP Objectives: Defend when outnumbered.

ORGANISATION
Two teams of four play in a zone that takes up the space of half a court. This playing area is then bisected by a horizontal line to create two separate zones. At the end of each zone is a mini goal.

Teams must defend their two mini goals while aiming to score in either of the two mini goals they are attacking. They must do so by setting up with two players in one half of the playing area and two players in the other half. When defending, the two players must stay in their zone. However, the attacking team is allowed to have three players in one zone at any one time. They can then only score with a first-time finish in either mini goal.

Teams should aim to switch play to create overloads with a numerical advantage. Here they can then connect and combine, or utilize techniques such as blocks and screens to create scoring opportunities.

PROGRESSIONS
- Allow players unlimited touches to score with

- Widen the playing areas to emphasize switching the play and using the four lanes
- Let the defending team also have a third player who can cross into the other zone, leaving a 1v1 in one of the zones

COACHING POINTS
Before Phase –
- How can players get on the ball?
- Assess when and how to join in from the other zone (are the players under severe pressure, for example?), recognizing the opportunity to finish the attack

During Phase –
- Selection of pass to quickly take advantage of the extra player by switching the play
- Finish first time
- Use 2v2 combinations
- Defending capabilities, both when 2v2 and when overloaded. How can defenders minimize danger?

After Phase –
- Ability to offer another quick passing angle to finish the attack or to support if there is good pressure on the ball

LINKS TO FOOTBALL
Good for quick, sharp passing when you have an extra player to finish attacks in and around the final third.

4-0 UP

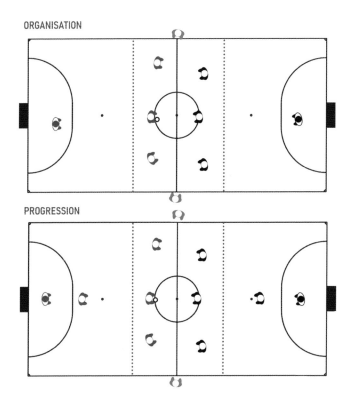

Number of Players: 8+2 goalkeepers

Equipment: 2 goals, balls, bibs, cones

IP Objectives: Understand key principles of the 4-0 system.

OOP Objectives: Keep pressure on the ball when underloaded.

ORGANISATION
A middle section is marked out on a full court. In this section a 3v3 takes place. On each sideline a floater is ready to play with the in possession team.

Once the ball reaches a floater, they have two touches with which to play. Here they have three options. They can play a pass forward into the attacking half for the in possession team to run onto and finish. Alternatively, they can play safe and set a player who drops into the defensive half. The team's job is then to use combination play to beat the defence. The final option is to simply play the ball back into the middle section.

PROGRESSIONS
• Add two defenders. These defend against attacking teams when they break into the attacking half. If they win possession

they recycle the ball to the team that was previously defending

COACHING POINTS
Before Phase –
- Body shape to open up the court and be able to play in any direction
- Recognize passing options before receiving the ball
- Assess pressure on the ball
- See whether there is cover – if not then the forward run is on. If there is and the defensive pressure is good, it may be best to retreat into the defensive half for a set back
- Set up with strongest foot open to the court to keep options open. Left-footers typically set up on the right and vice versa

During Phase –
- Awareness of teammates' positions
- Combination play using floaters, such as wall passes, parallel passes, diagonals

- Flatten out the opponents to exploit the space in behind
- Use of all four lanes

After Phase –
- Attacking movements in transition – which player balances, which goes to the second post, which provides support?
- Reaction to actions

LINKS TO FOOTBALL
When football teams defend as a compact unit, it becomes necessary to attack them in wide areas. This exercise emphasizes combination play in wide areas and mimics midfielders playing with wingers, creating chances following 2v2 and 3v3s. It also shows that inviting pressure from an opponent can be a positive as it creates space that can be exploited in behind. This is particularly important for football teams who seek to play out from the back. It encourages players to enjoy being pressed and maintain confidence on the ball.

PRINCIPLES OF IN POSSESSION PLAY IN THE FINAL THIRD

Create and Score

All of the principles discussed so far are important, but without the ability to score they become redundant. When it comes to creating and scoring there are three key areas, as illustrated in the Position of Maximum Opportunity (POMO) triangle covering the D and running up to the 10m penalty spot.

The aim for any team is to create the opportunity to score by penetrating or overloading the opponent with combination play, 1v1s and sets to finish.

When an attacker shoots, it is essential that they **finish the attack**. Ideally, this means

scoring a goal. However, if the attacker cannot score, it is vital that they win a set-piece, the ball passes the touchline or the keeper parries the ball back into a dangerous area. If the attack is not finished – perhaps because the shot is too weak or the pass is intercepted – then the attacking team becomes vulnerable to the counter-attack. Indeed, many teams are at their most vulnerable when they are attacking, due to the fact that they are seeking to overload their opponents. If the attack breaks down then attackers immediately have to turn around and run back toward their goal. This process is a lot slower than it is for opponents, who will be able to run forward and should have no need to turn. If the opponents are able to counter-attack, they are likely to be able to do so with an overload due to this difference in speed.

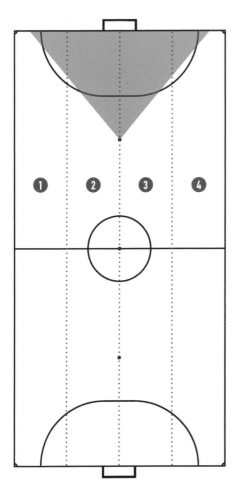

The Position of Maximum Opportunity triangle is located within the attacking third, specifically placed where most of the goals in futsal are scored.

To increase the chances of success when creating and scoring, there are a series of coaching points to pass on to your players.

- **Get the ball into the attacking tri-angle:** The highest player secures the ball and looks for the set back or the back post finish.
- **Finish first time:** Be ruthless with your finishing. Don't allow the keeper time to set or the defence time to react. If you take more than one touch in the D you're often smothered.
- **Second post top of D:** Make sure the player in possession always has two options: the final ball should go toward the second post (increasing the chances of a tap-in) or be set back to the top of the D, unless the player in possession can shoot. Players should be providing options in both places, making it harder to defend and opening up more passing lines.
- **Shoot high and hard:** Powerful strikes are tough for keepers to catch, reducing the chance of the attack being countered. Keepers favour split saves – where they spread their legs wide – meaning it's better to shoot high where less of the goal is covered.
- **Finish the attack:** Build pressure on opponents by limiting their chances to counter and develop a siege mentality on their goal and limit counter-attacks.

It is essential that opponents do not counter on an unfinished attack. If the attacker and passer are in the final phase and the opposite goalkeeper catches the ball, essentially 50 per cent (two players) of your team are out of the game, meaning an easy overload for the goalkeeper to initiate.

The ideal decision is guided by where the player is located within the attacking third.

Note 'security behind the ball'. When attacking, one of the outfield players needs to control the court and provide cover in case the action isn't finished, the attack breaks down and the team enters negative transition. This player also acts as a safe pass in case the defending team presses the attackers well and forces them backwards.

SESSION PLANS

The following sessions are designed to work on creating and scoring. Key coaching points are detailed, along with extra information to help you get the most out of each session.

A great number of futsal goals are scored at the second post.

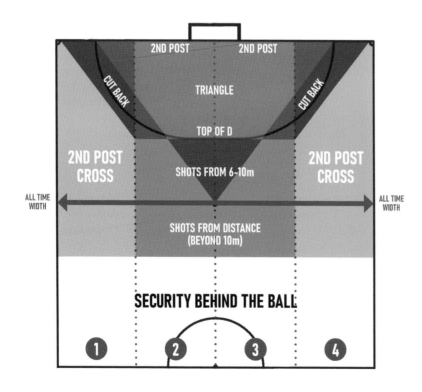

How and where to finish in the attacking third.

GOALS, GOALS, GOALS

FOCUS: Progressing the Game to Finish at Goal

ORGANISATION

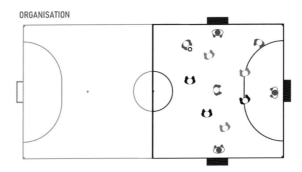

Number of Players: 12 (3v3v3+3 goalkeepers)

Equipment: 3× goals, balls, bibs (3 different colours)

IP Objectives: Recognize when to play and when to finish.

OOP Objectives: Understanding when and how to press while defending space with good pressure, cover and balance.

ORGANISATION

In a half-court area, players are split into three teams of three. Each team is also allocated a goal and a goalkeeper. To start, two teams keep possession while one defends. If the defending team wins the ball back by interception or simply kicking the ball off court, they get to attack and the team that lost possession becomes the defending team. When the in possession teams have made a set number of passes (we recommend eight), they can attack the defending team's goal.

PROGRESSIONS
- Play two touch
- Play 4v4v4
- Alter the number of passes required before finishing: ten passes would make for less finishing while four passes would see more finishing

COACHING POINTS
Before Phase –
- Players need to recognize where the space is to keep possession
- Players need to understand when to risk possession to try to score (don't rush it, just wait for the right movement – even if the required number of passes has been made)

During Phase –
- Change angle of attack if necessary
- Change the tempo of the attack
- Quality of technical passing to keep the ball (6v3)
- Quality of finishing at goal from 10–12m on average

After Phase –
- Support for progressing and finishing the game (sets back, second post finishes)
- Moving into negative transition in 3v6

LINKS TO FOOTBALL
Teams need to keep possession with a purpose, rather than possession for possession's sake. Measuring risk versus reward and analysing when to take a chance is key. For the out of possession team, working hard and smart as a pressing three is needed across the pitch.

MORE GOALS

ORGANISATION

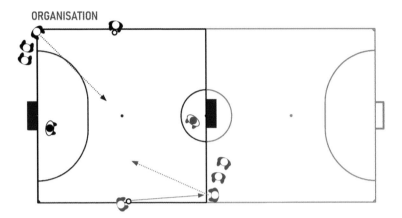

Number of Players: 10+2 goalkeepers

Equipment: 2× goals, balls, bibs

IP Objectives: Finish quickly in 1v1 scenarios.

OOP Objectives: Apply pressure quickly and stop the shot.

ORGANISATION

With one goal brought to the halfway line to create a 20×20m playing area, teams are split into two. Each team has a server who starts on the sideline. The red team's server starts the practice by passing to a teammate, who must then attempt to score in the goal they are attacking. As soon as the pass is played, an opposing blue defender is allowed to run into the playing area from the opposite corner to try to stop the goal.

After the first phase, the two players stay in the playing area. The blue server then passes to a teammate. As this pass is made, a red defender is allowed to enter, making a 2v2.

This is repeated after each action until the game is 4v4. The practice then finishes on a final action.

When the practice resets, the blue team gets to go first.

PROGRESSIONS
- Allow for goals in transition
- After the initial 1v1, all other goals must be scored with a first-time finish
- Allow kick-ins or corners as part of the practice (but not at the same time)

COACHING POINTS
Before Phase –
- Assess the space available and the movements of the approaching defender

During Phase –
- 1v1 skills of staying on the ball – finishing against an individual
- Can they finish before the defender engages?
- Dribbling techniques to beat a player

- Shooting and finishing skills with hard shots, side-foot finishes or quick fire toe-pokes
- Combining quickly with teammates in final third to score

After Phase –
- Movement to support teammate after action in order to get on the ball again
- Reaction to losing the ball and transitioning to becoming the defender

LINKS TO FOOTBALL
Quick combinations in and around the box to finish against matched-up opponents help to unlock football teams. This exercise is also great for defenders dealing with twisting and turning in tight areas.

1V1 DRIBBLING

FOCUS: Progress the Ball by Isolating and Then Beating a Defender

ORGANISATION

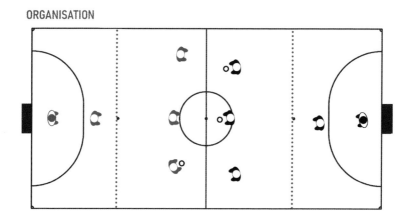

Number of Players: 10+

Equipment: 2× goals, balls, bibs

IP Objectives: To recognize when and where space is available to go 1v1.

OOP Objectives: 1v1 defensive principles such as pressing the strong foot, showing the opponent one way and reacting on triggers.

ORGANISATION
A pitch is split into thirds – the biggest third being the middle one. This is to allow more space for 1v1 duels. Players are split evenly into two teams. Each team has one goalkeeper and one defender in their defensive third. The rest of the players set up in the middle area.

The game begins on the coach's call. Each pair in the middle has a ball between them and when the coach calls, the 1v1 begins. A player can only score by dribbling the ball into the final third, where they are met by the opponent's covering defender. Once in the attacking third, the attacker must attempt to score, whether that's shooting before the covering defender can react, creating a yard of space or beating this defender too.

When the action finishes, the attacker then becomes the defender and the defensive team attacks.

PROGRESSIONS

- Play with more pairs in the middle to create more opportunities for blocks
- Use a floater in the middle to work on combination play

COACHING POINTS

Before Phase –

- Ability to find space to get on the ball to then travel forwards with it
- Seeing space to attack

During Phase –

- 1v1 skills to dribble or travel with the ball
- Attacking the space to get into the final third as quickly as possible
- Staying on the ball to develop attacking actions
- Finishing over the goal line in the final third

After Phase –

- Transitioning into defensive role after action

LINKS TO FOOTBALL

This is great for attacking players who like to dribble and drive at players but need more end product. It also helps attacking players to understand their defensive duties quickly as they can't switch off after finishing their attacking action. This develops transitional behaviours.

SINGLE OR DOUBLE

FOCUS: Create and Score in 1v1s and 2v2s

ORGANISATION

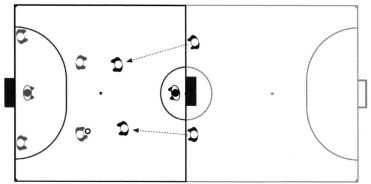

PROGRESSION

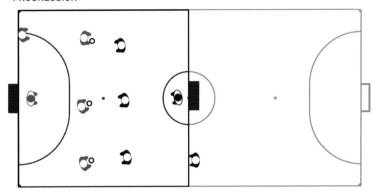

Number of Players: 10 (8+2 goalkeepers)

Equipment: 2× goals, balls, bibs

IP Objectives: To develop and acquire principles of spatial awareness and staying on the ball, along with connecting and combining to finish.

OOP Objectives: To develop principles of defending as an individual with core skills and laterality, emphasizing the need to press the stronger foot of the attacker.

ORGANISATION

In a 20×20m area with two goals, players play in two sets of 1v1s at the same time. This means there are two balls in play – one for each attacker. The practice starts when the goalkeeper rolls the balls out to one team, who then attempt to score in the opposite goal with both balls. Defenders must start on their own goal line and run to close down the attackers as the ball rolls. Defenders cannot change the player they are defending against. Play turns over when a goal is scored or the ball is won by the defending team.

PROGRESSIONS

- Play as a wave with a certain amount of balls with one team, for example, how many goals can they score with ten balls (in five attacks)?

- The ball can be dribbled into the game by the attacker, rather than the game starting when the goalkeeper rolls the ball
- Once one attacker strikes at goal, they can then join the other attacker to turn their 1v1 into a 2v1. A further progression would see the defender join their team-mate to turn it into a 2v2
- Add an extra player into the middle, making it 3v3 (in three sets of 1v1s)

COACHING POINTS: 2V2 COMBINATIONS
Before Phase –
- 1v1 skills of spatial awareness – how can a player create space for themselves?

During Phase –
- 1v1 skills of staying on the ball – can the player face forwards and commit to an attack, engaging the defender?
- Dribbling techniques to beat a player: can they deceive the defender, lure them in and roll them?
- Shooting and finishing skills: hard shots, side-foot finishes or quick-fire toe-pokes that finish the action

After Phase –
- Movement to support your teammate once the action finishes. Can you block the defender to create space for your teammate?

LINKS TO FOOTBALL

This exercise helps players to understand when and where to dribble. When isolated 1v1 in an offensive area, they have the highest chance of success. Here they are taught the spatial awareness required to operate at a high level, allowing them to attack in tight areas with an end product. Football, like futsal, is a game of 1v1s. These skills are essential for success in both sports. Defensively, it helps players to learn core skills such as attacking the strong foot of their opponent and using body shape to their advantage.

TAKING ADVANTAGE

FOCUS: Recognize Space to Attack 1v1

ORGANISATION

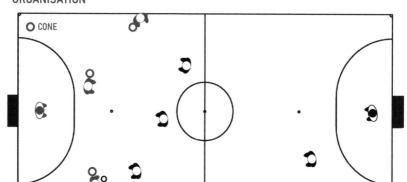

Number of Players: 10+ (minimum of 8+2 goalkeepers)

Equipment: 2× goals, balls, bibs (3 colours)

IP Objectives: Recognize when and where to go 1v1, taking advantage of an isolated defender.

OOP Objectives: Press 1v1, forcing the attacker in one direction. Recognize space and recover quickly if beaten.

ORGANISATION

On a full court, two teams take part in a normal game where both teams can score. One team starts with a cone each in their hand. If they want to take advantage of the situation (1v1) they can throw the cone on the floor within a metre of the opposite defender. The defender *must* pick it up before they can recover and defend. This is the attacker trying to take advantage and recognizing they have the space to attack goal. The player can also pass and play the game as normal with their teammates if they believe the dribble isn't on.

When the defender picks up the cone, that cone becomes theirs to use when the defending team win the ball back for them to take advantage. There are four cones in play at any one time (or one between two if playing with more or less players).

PROGRESSIONS
- Reduce the playing area to a 20×20m half court, making the space harder to take advantage of
- If a player takes advantage and the team fails to score in that possession they are removed from the game until the next goal is scored
- The team only plays with two cones (can even be reduced to just one)

COACHING POINTS
Before Phase –
- Players must face forward to see the space that they can take advantage of and then go past players

- Recognize where you and opponents are to take advantage
- Assess how far the goal is and the area of the court you are in (are you wide? Does the defender have cover, or is the team unbalanced?)

During Phase –
- Change of speed
- Change of direction
- Positive first touch
- End product to finish or set up goal

After Phase –
- Support next pass or recover to defend

LINKS TO FOOTBALL
1v1s happen all over the pitch in football. This teaches players when best to perform a 1v1, and also how best to defend it. In addition, it's a fun session that will help players to simply enjoy playing.

MAKE THE SPARES COUNT

FOCUS: Combining to Finish with an Overload

ORGANISATION

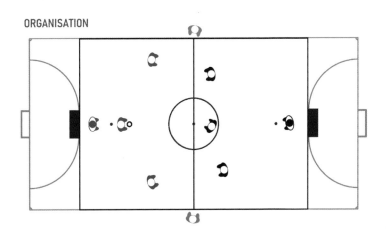

PROGRESSION

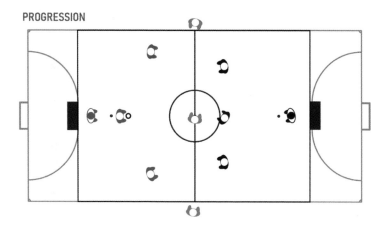

Number of Players: 8+2 goalkeepers

Equipment: 2× goals, balls, bibs

IP Objectives: Utilize the overload.

OOP Objectives: Work as a unit to limit the overload and protect the goal.

ORGANISATION

Players play in a 3v3 with a floater on each sideline. These floaters play for the in possession team and can move up and down the line as they please, making it a 5v3. Only first-time finishes count.

PROGRESSIONS

- Allow floaters to score from second post finishes
- Limit floaters to two touches
- Add an extra floater in the middle for combination play
- Floaters can be tackled
- When a player passes out to a floater they swap places
- Everyone limited to one touch

COACHING POINTS

Before Phase –

- Double movements to create space to get on the ball and face forward
- Movement to finish first time
- Quick support to switch the play and move the defensive three

During Phase –

- Pass forward
- Make forward runs to combine
- Use the spare players to overload the opponent
- Assess where the space is

After Phase –

- Support to finish first time depending on the pressure
- Occupy good areas to get rebounds/ deflections

LINKS TO FOOTBALL

Joy can often be found in wide areas – particularly when a winger or full back plays a wall pass centrally to then receive and cross. This also encourages attackers to position themselves in areas of maximum opportunity, such as the back post and top of the D.

1V1 MAYHEM

ORGANISATION

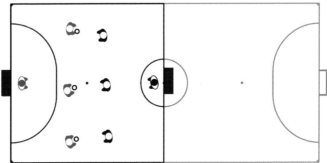

Number of Players: 6+2 goalkeepers

Equipment: 2× goals, balls, bibs (3 colours)

IP Objectives: To finish in a 1v1 situation by recognizing when and where the space is.

OOP Objectives: To defend 1v1, then transition quickly to attack.

ORGANISATION
One goal is brought forward to the halfway line, shortening the length of the court but maintaining its width. In this reduced playing area, players are split into two teams of three. Each player is then paired with an opponent. They play against each other in a 1v1 on the same court at the same time, each pair with their own ball. Goalkeepers must do their best to stop any shot coming their way and then recycle the ball for their team once the action is over.

PROGRESSIONS
- Add extra pairs
- Increase the size of the court
- Take a ball away to leave 3v3 with two balls

- Add a floater who can combine with any attacking players

COACHING POINTS
Before Phase –
- Movement to get on the ball from the goalkeeper
- Face forwards when receiving to attack instantly

During Phase –
- 1v1 skills of staying on the ball and facing forwards
- Dribbling techniques to beat a player
- Shooting and finishing skills with hard shots, side-foot finishes or quick-fire toe-pokes

After Phase –
- Movement to defend against a 1v1

LINKS TO FOOTBALL
Good game for youth players that is physically demanding and therefore good for conditioning. Excellent to develop 1v1 perception skills around attacking and exploiting space.

DEVELOPING 2V2S – PULPIS

FOCUS: Paired Movements to Finish

Jose Pazos ('Pulpis') is a Spanish coach who is currently in charge of Benfica in Portugal and was the head coach of the Thailand national team. He is also a FIFA Instructor and a UEFA Technical Observer. In this exercise, he explores paired movements (dualities), progressing into pivot play.

ORGANISATION

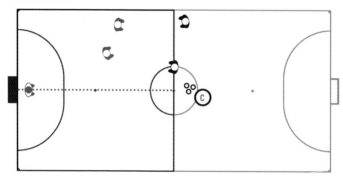

PROGRESSION

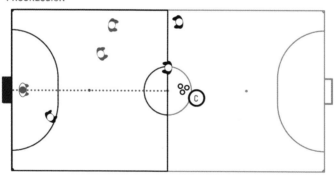

Number of Players: 4+ with a goalkeeper

Equipment: Goal, balls, bibs, cones

IP Objectives: Understand how paired movements can unlock space and create forward opportunities.

OOP Objectives: Press, cover and balance in order to win the ball back and transition over the halfway line.

ORGANISATION
Two attacking players set up on the halfway line with two defenders up against them. The exercise begins when the goalkeeper throws the ball to either of the attackers, who must then combine in the attacking half to score. The half they are attacking in is further bisected by a central vertical line, meaning the attackers must stay within one half of this attacking half. If the ball goes out of play then the defenders

become the attackers and the attackers become the defenders.

PROGRESSIONS
- Only allow defenders to change to the attacking role if they win the ball and transition over the halfway line
- Consider playing 2v1
- Place a pivot or forward player to support and join in once the defenders' line has been beaten or to open the diagonal pass

COACHING POINTS
Before Phase –
- Timing of movement to receive the ball
- Runs forward, facing forward
- Double movements (one to shift the defender, one to exploit the space)
- Blocks and screens

During Phase –
- Working with the different possibilities of paired movements (wall pass, helping pass, parallel pass with corner runs and diagonal pass)

After Phase –
- Getting into position quickly again to receive and play an attacking pass

LINKS TO FOOTBALL
Vertical and horizontal combinations happen all over the football pitch, particularly in the final third and wide areas. This exercise is a fantastic way to develop a player's understanding with a teammate.

IN SUMMARY

The attacking principles discussed in this chapter can be summarized as:

- Dominate possession and territory
- Look forward, play forward
- Show control and patience
- Attack across four lanes
- Create and score

By splitting the court into horizontal and vertical lines, it becomes easier to understand so that you can teach these principles to your players. Ultimately, these players must work to overload the opposition so that they can dominate the court, create space and penetrate opponents, leading to shooting opportunities.

Remember, these are only guidelines – a framework to develop from. There is still plenty of room for individual freedom and maverick play. As a coach, you provide players with the knowledge of how to attack, why to attack, where to attack and when to attack. The rest is down to them on the court.

Now that the attacking principles have been covered, it is time to move onto a part of the game that is equally important for any team: out of possession principles.

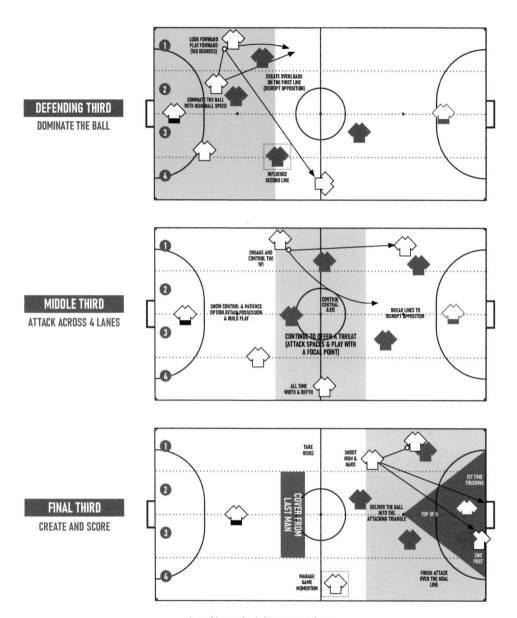

DEFENDING THIRD

DOMINATE THE BALL

MIDDLE THIRD

ATTACK ACROSS 4 LANES

FINAL THIRD

CREATE AND SCORE

Attacking principles summed up.

3 OUT OF POSSESSION

At times it can feel impossible for teams to break down a rigid, organised defence. And in theory, if a team stays organised, denies space and presses effectively and in synchronisation, they should not concede a goal. In this chapter, we'll share the key principles that make a team solid in defence, giving them the foundations to go forward and use the ball effectively.

First, we must consider out of possession to be made up of five distinct principles:

- Pressure on the ball and counter pressing
- Compactness and closing the middle
- Dominate 1v1
- Defending special teams (to be detailed in Chapter 5)
- Defending set-play excellence (to be detailed in Chapter 6)

When applying these principles, teams will choose to organise themselves in set formations.

There are a range of different defensive set-ups, each with their advantages and disadvantages. Regardless of which set formation a team chooses, it is important that they always maintain three lines of defence, in addition to the keeper acting as the ultimate line of defence. As with the attacking threshold concepts, individual defending skills are the foundations of any good team structure, with the way that you defend in pairs paramount to how the team will defend collectively.

The greater the number of the lines of the defence, the more challenging it is for attackers to penetrate a team. With multiple lines of defence, there is cover and balance in case a defender is dribbled past, the opponents combine with a wall pass or similar, or a pass cuts through the team. A defending team should therefore seek to occupy as many lines as possible within any system or positional defence and with as much pressure, cover and balance as five players can achieve.

Working together to win the ball back.

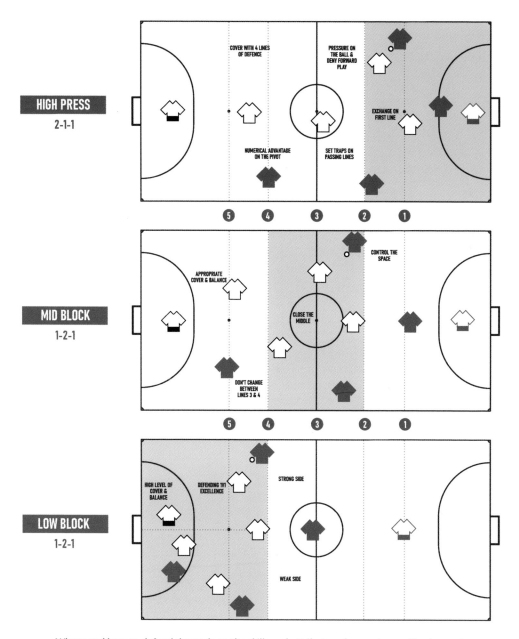

Where and how to defend depends on the skills and attributes of your players, the demands and states of the game and the opposition.

WHERE TO ENGAGE

With England and in club futsal, it was always the ambition to maintain three lines of defence by using several systems, which players are encouraged to switch between dependent on their skills and attributes, the demands and state of the game and the

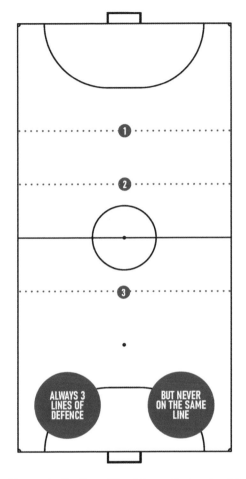

The greater the lines of the defence, the tougher it is for an opponent to penetrate.

The five lines of defence indicate where the first line of pressure engages an opponent.
Lines 1 and 2: Pressing.
Lines 2 and 3: Mid block.
Lines 3 and 4: Low block.
Line 5: Low block (special situation).

opposition's weaknesses (not their strengths). In a mid block, for example, the second and third lines of pressure would typically be on lines 4 and 5.

HIGH PRESS (1-1-2, THOUGH SOMETIMES 1-2-1)

As is implied by its name, the high press requires a team to defend high up the court. The highest positioned players must **apply** **intense pressure on the ball**, ideally at either line 1 or 2. Rather than charge off as soon as the ball is set down, a player must only apply intense pressure once their teammates can move in synchronisation, working as a unit to limit a player's options and force a mistake. If successful, this means the team will win the ball back high up the court and close to the opponent's goal, increasing the chance of a successful counter-attack.

The two players on line 1 press aggressively. The closest player to the ball presses the ball,

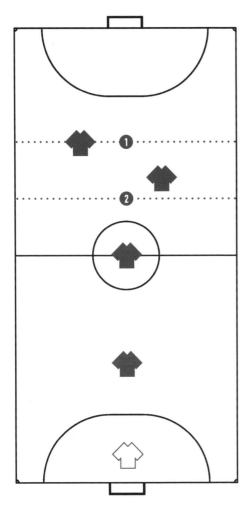

The high press method of defending.

defender is the insurance policy, preventing the ball into the pivot while offering protection in case both of the top lines are breached. These two deeper players must communicate, particularly if any teammate should track an opponent and call out any exchanges.

Ramp up the Pressure

In football, defenders are encouraged to get 'touch-tight'. This means they should be an arm's length from the player with the ball. In futsal, players should get even closer. They can further intimidate opponents by making themselves appear bigger, such as by moving their arms out to the side. Physical contact with the opponent is encouraged so long as it does not exceed what is legal. This will blunt their acceleration, just one reason why applying physical contact that is just inside what is considered legal is known in the business as 'the dark arts'. Getting so close can be risky, which is why defenders should watch an opponent's hips or even eyes: these give great clues as to what an opponent is planning to do next.

If a defender is unable to get to the opposition player in possession in time, they should instead pressurize forward passing lines. As the ball then moves sideways or backwards, a teammate should be able to get better pressure on the ball.

Throughout this system, there has to be constant second line cover. This means that if the high pressing defending line is breached, the next line can either delay the opponent until the first line of defence has recovered back into position, or simply deny them the space by making the court small and forcing their opponent in one direction (ideally onto their weaker foot and away from other attackers while closing the middle). This will help to create numerical superiority, which

while the second attacker closes off the sideways pass. It's very important they maintain their vertical position, even if their opponent runs off. The system requires bravery and the ability to anticipate a different opponent rotating back into the space. The middle player provides cover, controlling the centre of the court to block diagonal passes and get across to any opponent able to break the first line of defence with a pass or dribble. The deepest is especially important when defending the opponent's pivot.

If any line of defence is breached, the defenders must turn and get back into position behind the ball as quickly as possible. This (recovery runs) is one of the first individual principles of defence.

KITE (3-1 MID BLOCK)

The Kite differs from a high press by engaging the opponent slightly lower, on lines 2 or 3.

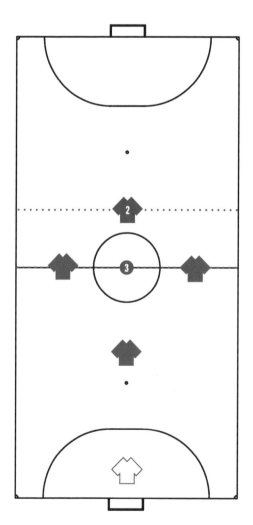

The kite method of defending.

The highest point of the defensive unit is just over the halfway line. Again, it is important that intense pressure is applied on opponents, but only once they enter the lines of engagement. If this pressure is then good, it can be maintained even if an opponent moves back toward their own goal (past line 1).

In this system of defence, **identifying and developing triggers** is essential. These 'triggers' are cues that an attacker is not comfortable in possession and can be dispossessed with intense pressure. Such triggers include:

- If the attacker is taking multiple touches on the ball, known as 'slow play'.
- If the attacker has their back to the goal.
- If the ball is on the attacker's weak side.
- If the attacker is on their weak side on court (if a left-footed player is on the left side, for example).
- A slow pass.
- A pass backwards.
- Hips are facing backwards or sideways.

Once these triggers are identified, a player should try to apply intense pressure. If this is successful, their teammates should 'lock on' to the other attackers. This is to increase the chances of winning possession. If the defender is doing a good job, they will either win the ball themselves or severely limit the attacker's passing options. This will then build pressure on the opponent and help to force a mistake.

Once a team becomes competent at recognizing triggers they can learn how to set pressing traps on the first line of defence and even develop into sophisticated methods of defence, such as exchanging opponents on the first line to maintain pressure on the ball and allow fast forward pressure.

This is where the futsal concept pyramid is not only important for in possession but also out of possession.

In the Kite, constant cover must be provided to the first defender to balance the team.

Hunt as a Pack

There is no point pressing if only one defender recognizes a trigger and applies intense pressure. That's because the player that is pressed will likely still have some options open. If they then pass to these options who are not pressed, it is easy for the opponent to keep possession. When all defenders press together, using the good pressure on the ball as their own trigger to get tight and make it tough for opponents, it increases the likelihood of winning the ball. When this happens, it is important that deeper players provide cover to prevent diagonal passes into space and to exchange runners in behind. This allows a team to maintain their vertical positions, which keeps the pressure on the opponent. Building pressure as a team is key.

Staying in Shape

When defending as a diamond it is important to understand that the diamond shape is always in reference to where the ball is on the court. So when the ball is on the wings, the defensive diamond might actually look like a box, even though the diamond shape is maintained: the wide player applies the first pressure rather than the top player.

Diamond Defence (1-2-1 low block)

A Diamond Defence – or 1-2-1 – seeks to protect the team's own half. It allows the opponent to play in their own half (until pressure is good and players can lock on) but reduces the amount of space for the opposition in central areas (lines 3 and 4). As with the other formations, three lines of defence are maintained, yet given the space available this set-up is effective at reducing the number of forward passes available to the opponent. Limiting the space for the attacking team enables high levels of cover and balance on the strong side of court. Any forward passes that do cut through the defence, or any dribbles past players, are dangerous and will likely result in a chance to finish. 1v1 excellence and compact shape are of major importance in this defensive system. Given the space available to run into if possession is regained, however, there is also an increased chance of a greater number of attacking transitions.

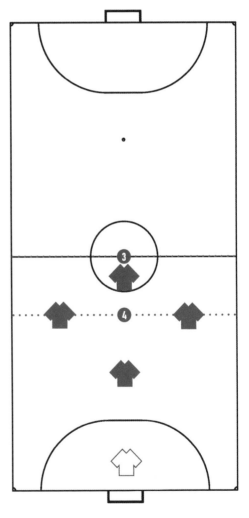

The diamond method of defending.

Regardless of the system used, the team principles of out of possession play remain the same.

HOW TO DEFEND?

There are defensive structures based around organising the team in defence and positional defending as a team. These can be known as the system within the player concept pyramid.

Within that, there are four main ways of defending as a team.

- Player for player – A type of defensive play where every player has individual responsibility and is required to mark or lock on to one of the opposition players.
- Zonal defence – A type of defensive action where players are required to defend their space rather than a player and ultimately each player is required to defend opposition players when they are in their area or zone.
- Mixed defence – A type of defence that has some players zonal defending and some players man for man marking. This could be seen like a basketball team who deny the point guard the ball, for example.
- Exchanging or switching defence – This is a player for player marking defence where players pass on or change players depending on the team principles, strategy and structure. This defence needs to be based on high-level decision-making and team understanding.

Once the structure has been decided, teams should look to build their defence with the following in mind:

Pressure on the Ball – When a defender gets good pressure on the ball it presents a trigger for teammates to read and react in their defensive decisions and actions. It is important to coach players' perception of these situations so that they can make good decisions as to when to cover or press.

Compactness/Closing the Middle – As a team principle it is key to control the centre of the court with and without the ball, stopping any attacks in the middle of your structure. Achieve this with good individual defending, paired defending and overall team structure.

Dominate 1v1 and Control the Space – This could be in a 1v1 situation or buying time by stalling or slowing the attack down. It also includes withdrawal; recovery runs behind the ball where defenders never lose sight of the ball as they recover.

If these principles are done well, they should be reinforced with the stability of three lines of defence. This helps to stop forward play and limits the damage an opponent can do in one move.

If the out of possession objectives are then successfully achieved, a team should regain possession, prevent the opponents from invading their space and ultimately prevent the other team from scoring.

Pressing to Stop Forward Play

Within the principle of pressing, there are five further sub principles that enable a defending team to prevent forward passes and enhance their ability to regain possession.

Counter Pressing to Stop Forward Play: When the ball is lost, the closest defender to the ball should react first. A team should aim to win the ball back as quickly as possible. If they cannot, then they should revert to their organised defensive set-up. This is also a common tactic in football, with coaches such as Jurgen Klopp asking their players to win the ball back within six seconds of losing it.

Set Traps and React to Pressing Triggers: As discussed in the Kite system of defence, triggers are cues that help a defending team to win the ball back in ideal

Minimizing space to turn in.

scenarios. 'Traps' encourage opponents to show 'triggers'. An example of a trap could be the defender on the first line of pressure angling their body shape so that the opponent must pass in a certain direction. This telegraphs what is about to happen next to the other defenders, who can start to creep up and apply the pressure. If the pass is made to a player on their weak side, or the pressure is good enough that the attacker must take a touch backwards or sideways, the trap has been set and the trigger has been displayed. The pressurizing defender should then press the opponent's weak foot, making them more uncertain and less confident of escaping the pressure. Further triggers are on display when a player is in possession. A defender should look at the position of the opponent's hips and the line of their eyes to anticipate what is about to

happen next. By forcing their opponent in a certain direction, they are making play predictable, which allows the other defenders to react accordingly.

Always Three Lines of Defence: These three lines are in place to restrict space and deny passes. Players should feel comfortable exchanging opponents as they move on the first line. This means that the defender on line 1 holds their position and defends a new attacker who rotates toward them. If unsure, always follow the opponent in a player-to-player system (a teammate should shout if they want to exchange) – even if it compromises the three lines of defence. While defending, players should always maintain their defensive triangle. This means that they are able to see the opponent they are marking and the ball at all times.

Control the Centre of the Court with Cover and Balance: When the attackers have the ball in the centre of the court it is dangerous due to the amount of options they have and passing lines that are open. Defenders need to recognize danger, such as when a player is about to shoot or pass forward, and react accordingly.

Regain with Intelligence: It is not always possible to regain possession. A defender should only attempt to regain the ball when it is realistic to do so – especially given that each team can only commit five fouls per half. Failure to steal the ball can result in the defender selling themselves, costing the whole team and risking an overload.

Intelligent defenders therefore attack the passing lane and player, jump to the next attacker if the ball moves less than 5yd and they remain the closest defender, exhibiting top 1v1 defending skills at all times. This jumping is a tactic within a defensive structure to put pressure on the ball. While it is effective, some coaches may prefer not to use it.

SESSION PLANS

The following sessions are designed to work on pressing. Key coaching points are detailed, along with extra information to help you get the most out of each session.

CONTROL THE COURT

FOCUS: Defensive Skills of Pressing, Cover, Floating and Peripheral Vision

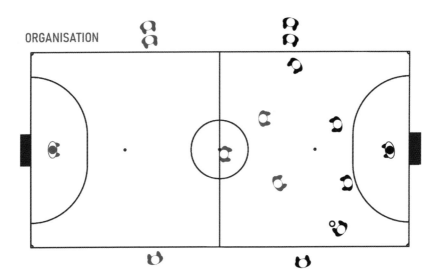

Number of Players: 8+ with 2 goalkeepers

Equipment: 2 goals, balls, bibs

IP Objectives: Quick combination play to progress possession past the halfway line and escape the press.

OOP Objectives: Deny forward play by defending on different lines and controlling the court to remove the disadvantage of the underload.

ORGANISATION
On a full court, a game takes place between two teams. The defending team must defend with just three players, while the attacking team is allowed to attack with four. The attacking team must start in their own half and make three passes before they are allowed to cross the halfway line. The defending team must press the attackers in order to prevent this.

If the attacking team get over the halfway line then they are free to score. The defending team should recover as quickly as possible and revert to defending in a low block. This 3v4 low block mimics the tactics for defending with a player sent off.

If the attackers lose possession of the ball then the player who lost the ball must immediately leave the court, with the attackers now acting as the defenders. They will have just three outfield players on court. A player is allowed to enter for the team previously defending, giving them four attackers. The scenario repeats, with the new attacking team needing to make three passes before they can cross the halfway line.

PROGRESSIONS
- Use as a warm-up with more players
- Increase the number of passes the attacking team must make before they can cross

the halfway line to further work on the defensive press

COACHING POINTS
Before Phase –
- Stop the forward pass and control the court
- When to press, where to press and how to press
- Recognizing which of the three defenders presses, which covers and which balances

During Phase –
- Recognize the opportunity to win the ball when matched up
- Defend passing lines
- Floating and spatial awareness as a defender
- Make play predictable – how to force the ball in one direction
- Invade and win the ball back

After Phase –
- Reset the press
- Work as a unit in the first and second lines of the press
- Communicate the change to the low block
- Positive transition from defence to attack

LINKS TO FOOTBALL
Modern football teams press from the front. This puts responsibility on forward players to win the ball back. The higher they win the ball back, the closer they are to goal. This therefore gives them a better chance of scoring. By working on this aspect of the game, forwards understand the importance of stopping forward passes, pressing the ball and pressing passing lines. It also allows them to sense opportunities to win the ball back with numerical balance. Meanwhile, a high press magnifies the importance of the keeper and their ability to protect their own defensive half as a 'sweeper keeper'.

THE SWEEPER

FOCUS: Defensive Skills of Pressing, Cover, Floating and Peripheral Vision

ORGANISATION

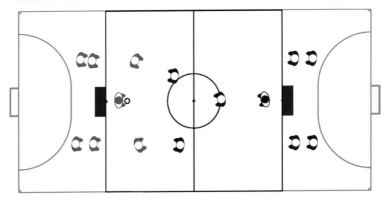

PROGRESSION

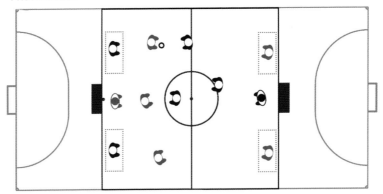

Number of Players: 9+ with 2 goalkeepers

Equipment: 2 goals, balls, bibs

IP Objectives: See forward passes or forward dribbles as quickly as possible.

OOP Objectives: Press as a pair with intensity on the first line of defence while trusting in the defensive cover.

ORGANISATION

Set out a 20×20m area with two goals. Each team has two lines of players behind their goal with a 2v2 in the defending half of the in possession team. The out of possession team is then able to add another defender into their own half to create an overall defensive overload.

If the ball is won by the defending team on the court then a quick transition occurs with an attacking overload. If the ball exits the court, the team that was in possession starts once again from their goalkeeper in a 2v3 underload.

Each time the out of possession team wins the ball and transitions, they may then exit the court and another set of players enters. When the in possession team lose the ball, the two players must remain on the court until they recover possession or score.

PROGRESSIONS
- Turn into a 3v3 game with pivots in end boxes working on the cover principles and stopping passing lines forward
- Turn into a 3v3 with floating players on the sidelines (emulating a 4-0) to create different passing lines for the defenders to stop

COACHING POINTS
Before Phase –
- Defenders press the ball quickly
- Block off passing lines and reduce opportunities to switch the play
- Can the covering defender block passing lines and provide balance?

During Phase –
- Work as a unit to either block the middle or block the line pass
- Press on triggers
- Stop the forward pass first

After Phase –
- Recognize the transition and react quickly
- Positive transition from defence to attack
- Reset if beaten: the covering defender now presses with the next closest defender joining them as the two pressing players

LINKS TO FOOTBALL
Increasingly in modern football, the team that is most aggressive off the ball is most successful. With high press also proving a popular tactic, players must be comfortable pressing quickly and putting opponents under rapid pressure. Taking responsibility to stop the forward pass is key. This exercise works on high reward pressing: if teams win the ball they are relieved of their defensive duties (which are also physically demanding).

A TRANSFER WITH A TRANSITION

FOCUS: Pressing Ability and Defensive Transition

ORGANISATION

PROGRESSION

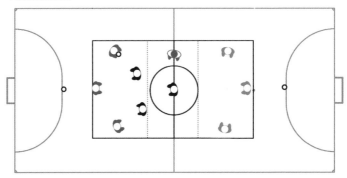

Number of Players: 9+

Equipment: Balls, bibs

IP Objectives: See forward passes as quickly as possible.

OOP Objectives: Press as a pair with intensity on the first line of defence.

ORGANISATION
Split a playing area into thirds. A 24×10m works well but can be adapted depending on age and ability. Three teams of three play within this area. The defending team sets up in the middle third while the two teams at either end are attacking. These attacking teams must stay in their third. Only the defending team is allowed to leave their third.

The attacking teams must make six passes in their third for a point. However, they can also transfer the ball across to the other attacking team in the opposite third to score a point. Two defenders from the defending team are allowed in the third where the ball is to stop this from happening. The remaining player provides balance and cover, attempting to intercept any passes that come through the middle zone.

If the defending team win the ball back then they can turn and play the ball to the other attacking team. This action releases them from their defensive duties. They switch places with the team that lost possession, who now become the defending team. If they do not win the ball back but it goes out of play then the two teams enter into a race. A ball is set up outside the playing area on the 10m penalty spot. Both teams must instantly transition to this ball. The defending team attempt to score with this ball while the attacking team must stop them. If the defending team is successful then they are released from their duties and switch places with the attacking team.

PROGRESSIONS
- Add a floater for the in possession teams. This floater can play between the lines in the middle third to support the attackers
- Alter the number of passes required to score a point
- Allow the in possession teams to transfer the ball by dribbling into the middle third then passing

COACHING POINTS
Before Phase –
- Defenders press the ball quickly, blocking off passing lines to make the 2v3 a 2v2 and even out the disadvantage
- The covering defender blocks passing lines, providing balance

During Phase –
- Work as a unit to either block the middle or block the line pass
- Press on triggers
- Stop the forward pass first
- Apply fast pressure if slow ball speed and negative body shape

LINKS TO FOOTBALL
Pressing aggressively is pointless without cover and balance. This exercise mimics forward players attempting to win the ball back high up the pitch while midfielders cut off passing lines and provide cover if the first line is broken.

After Phase –
- Recognize the transition and react quickly
- Positive transition from defence to attack
- Reset if beaten: the covering defender now presses with the next closest defender joining them as the pressing two players

2V2 TUNNEL

FOCUS: Pressing as a Pair

ORGANISATION

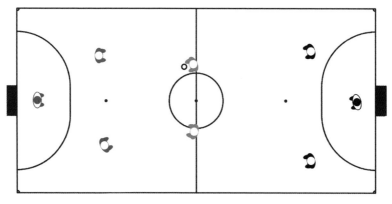

Number of Players: 8+ (with 2 goalkeepers)

Equipment: 2× goals, balls, bibs

IP Objectives: Take advantage of the 2v2 with positive touches, blocks and screens.

OOP Objectives: Press as a pair to prevent shots on goal.

ORGANISATION
Players are paired up. Two begin by defending one goal while another pair defends the other. These pairs are up against two attackers. The

coach begins the exercise by playing to one of the attackers, who are set up on the halfway line. These attackers then decide which goal to attack. Defenders cannot leave their half.

If the attackers score then they turn and attack the other goal. If they miss then the pair defending the goal just attacked become the attackers and attempt to score in the opposite goal.

PROGRESSIONS

- If the attacking team get a shot on target then they get to attack the other goal
- Play the game in threes rather than pairs
- Add an attacking floater
- Add a defensive floater to underload the attackers

COACHING POINTS

Before Phase –

- Understand timing, movement and space
- Anticipate the danger

During Phase –

- Press quickly – nearest player to the ball presses, the other covers
- Prevent attackers from facing forward
- Switch markers if necessary

After Phase –

- Positive transition

LINKS TO FOOTBALL

Football is played in pairs across the pitch, for example central midfielders, wingers and full backs. The court can be altered in this exercise to reflect this. If it's two central midfielders it can be wide, if a full back and winger then it can change to long and narrow. These pairs must attack together, but also defend together with one pressing while the other covers to prevent forward passes.

PRESS THE SWITCH – PULPIS

FOCUS: The Fundamentals of a Switch Defence

ORGANISATION

Number of Players: 6+ with 2 goalkeepers (ideally 9 so 3 can rest while the other 6 play)

Equipment: 2× goals, balls, bibs, cones

IP Objectives: Combination play between three players to advance possession.

OOP Objectives: Understand when to switch and when to follow in defence.

ORGANISATION

With the goals brought forward to the edge of the 6m area, a normal game takes place. There are three players on each team. The defensive team must press the ball. If their opponent rotates into a new area then the defenders must practise 'switching' who they mark.

If there is good pressure on the ball from the first player, then the second player on the first line tries to block passing lines and the furthest defender covers the player directly pressing the ball. If the ball is played forward the covering defender takes the player to get quick pressure on the ball and the defender previously trying to press the passing line switches and becomes the last covering defender.

PROGRESSIONS

- Give each team a set number of attacks to defend and see how well they defend the goal (for example, each team has ten balls to defend)

COACHING POINTS

Before Phase –

- The defending players must read the pressure on the ball to decide whether to follow the attacking runner or stay to pressure the passing line
- Defenders must also read the direction of the player on the ball and the game

orientation. Which way are their hips facing, for example?

During Phase –

- Work with the different possibilities of preventing paired movements. Can the defender block the passer's run with their body to slow them and make it harder for them to receive?
- Body shape to force play in one direction
- Communication to 'switch'
- Switches to take place when the deepest defender recognizes the rotation and calls for a teammate to switch and maintain their position
- Scanning to build pictures of the court

After Phase –

- Recovery runs (in straight lines for speed and efficiency)
- Working out which player needs to provide balance and cover
- The player now closest to the ball presses
- Getting into position quickly again to receive and play an attacking pass

LINKS TO FOOTBALL

Most football teams switch players when defending. When defending an overlap, for example, defenders must work out which one marks the oncoming attacker and which passing line to shut off. This helps players to understand defensive rotations. It could be the midfield three who want to try to keep pressure on the ball and not lose their screening roles. For example, if a holding midfielder has to come out to press, how does the centre midfielder furthest away from the ball take the most attacking players or screen the forward players to prevent passes forward?

READ THE CUES – MIGUEL RODRIGO

FOCUS: Pressing with Cover and Balance

ORGANISATION

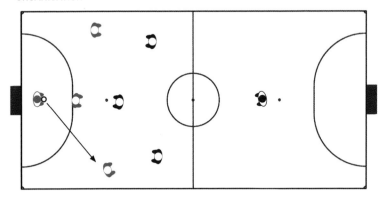

PROGRESSION

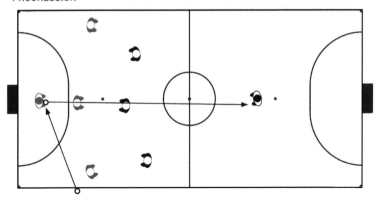

Number of Players: 6+ with 2 goalkeepers (ideally 9 so 3 can rest while the other 6 play)

Equipment: 2× goals, balls, bibs, cones

IP Objectives: Play through high-pressure scenarios with different speeds of cutting, connections and pivot passes, recognizing where the spatial advantage is.

OOP Objectives: Individual, paired and group defending to press on cues and cover accordingly.

ORGANISATION

On a full court, three reds set up in their defensive half. They are matched up by three blues who are pressing to win the ball back. The practice starts when the goalkeeper rolls the ball out to a red player. The reds must make at least two passes before they are allowed to cross the halfway line. If they do make it, they then go 1v1 against the opposition to try to score. If the defending team wins the ball then they must attempt to score as normal.

PROGRESSIONS

- Change the opposition goalkeeper with a pivot: the defending team must now stop the attackers from playing a long pass into the pivot
- Change the starting point from the goalkeeper to a kick-in
- The defenders must jump to the keeper when the ball is played, creating an underload

COACHING POINTS

Before Phase –

- Read the pressure on the ball to decide whether to follow the attacker as they move or stay to press the passing line
- Read the direction of the player on the ball and the game orientation

During Phase –

- Decisions to switch, follow or jump
- If a forward pass is made then the decision of whether to switch defensive roles with the player behind is key

After Phase –

- Recovery runs (in straight lines for speed and efficiency)
- Reapply good and strong pressure on the ball

LINKS TO FOOTBALL

High pressing on the first line of defence allows teams to win the ball back in dangerous areas where they are more likely to score. Meanwhile, working to cover and balance means that if the first line of defence is breached, the second line prevents an opponent from immediately scoring or progressing. This applies to football's minimum of three lines of defence: the forwards, midfielders and defenders.

PICK UP THE PRESSURE

FOCUS: Individual Pressure on the Ball

ORGANISATION

Number of Players: 4+ with 1 goalkeeper (ideally 8 players in a 4v4 with 1 goalkeeper)

Equipment: Goal, balls, bibs

IP Objectives: Quick combination play to escape pressure.

OOP Objectives: Get fast pressure on individuals in possession to regain the ball as quickly as possible.

ORGANISATION

All players on the half court have one ball in their hand, while there is one ball on the floor between everyone. The players are separated into two teams. The teams then enter into a possession game where ten consecutive passes equals one goal. The team in possession can also pass to the goalkeeper, who acts as a 'floating player'.

When possession turns over to the defending team, the score resets to zero. However, if any in possession player feels that the pressure they are being put under by an opponent is too much then they can simply chip the ball up into their hands. This is the trigger movement for one of their teammates to then put the ball in their hands down onto the floor. This ball then becomes the one that all players play with on the court. This also resets the in possession team's score to zero.

PROGRESSIONS

- The ball can be chipped into the keeper to count as a goal
- Play the game across the full court, rather than just in one half
- Add a second goalkeeper

COACHING POINTS

Before Phase –

- Track opponents unless a call comes to 'exchange'
- Dominate the court by stopping passing lines into players

During Phase –

- Get fast pressure on the ball to stop the pass into the goalkeeper
- Intercept if possible
- Press aggressively on triggers such as slow play

After Phase –

- React to defend another goal
- Read the pressure on the ball to double up (if pressure is good) or press passing lines more aggressively

LINKS TO FOOTBALL

Playing as a high pressing or counter pressing team requires individuals to get fast pressure on the ball. This exercise teaches players when to emphasize that pressure, such as on triggers, along with the correct way to press (on opponent's weak foot, forcing them in one direction and closer than touch-tight).

ALL ABOUT THE INDIVIDUAL – TIAGO POLIDO

FOCUS: Individual Defending

Tiago Polido is a Portuguese futsal coach who has won national championships in Italy and Croatia. More recently he's worked with Mumbai Warriors in India and Kamza SC in Kuwait.

ORGANISATION

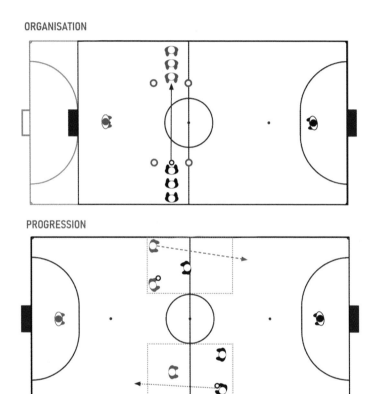

PROGRESSION

Number of Players: 3+

Equipment: Goal, balls, bibs

IP Objectives: Paired combination play.

OOP Objectives: Develop defensive body position and improve defensive laterality by using the body and arms in 1v1 defending.

ORGANISATION

The attacking players start the practice by entering through the gates. They then have one touch only to make ten passes before they can score in the goal. Guarding the goal is the defensive player who is allowed to engage from the 10m spot once the first pass is made.

If the attacking pair score a goal then the defender stays protecting the goal. If the attackers lose possession, however, the attacker who made the mistake becomes the new defender and must now protect the goal.

PROGRESSIONS
- Play 2v1 in a 15×7m rectangle with no limitation on the amount of touches attackers can take. If the attackers get past the defender and through the end line of the rectangle then they can attack the keeper, but with just one-touch passing and a first-time finish

COACHING POINTS
Before Phase –
- Get the defensive body position low to aid agility
- Use hands and get arms out for balance and to create a visual barrier for the attackers
- Read the body position and orientation of attackers to anticipate the next action

During Phase –
- Defensive feints
- Press the ball
- Use laterality to get pressure on the ball or cut out passing lines

After Phase –
- Recover in a straight line back to the goal

LINKS TO FOOTBALL
Pressing takes place all over the pitch. This practice is excellent for explaining pressing detail to defenders, particularly for when they press in the first line on the football pitch. Here they will learn how to press from out to in and in to out, along with emphasizing quick decisions to aid the timing of the press.

DOUBLE UP – TIAGO POLIDO

FOCUS: Defending as a Pair and in Small Units

ORGANISATION

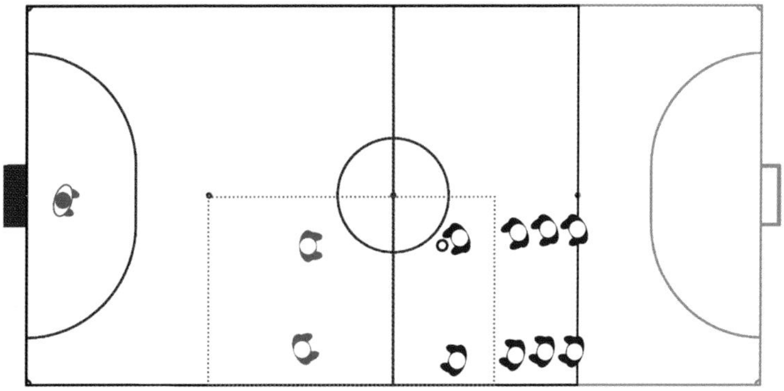

PROGRESSION

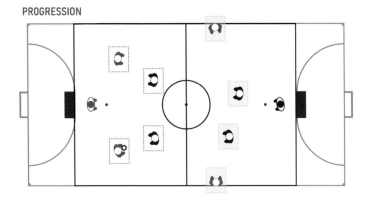

Number of Players: 8+ with 2 goalkeepers

Equipment: 2× goals, balls, bibs

IP Objectives: Paired combination to utilize overloads.

OOP Objectives: Develop the understanding of how to press an opponent's stronger leg, and potential passing lines. Alongside this, improving defensive jumping and covering when necessary.

ORGANISATION
The in possession players attack in a 20×10m box. If they are able to get out of the box they finish at goal, using just one-touch passing and one-touch finishing. The defenders only operate in the box. If a defender wins the ball back in the box then the attackers become the defenders and the defenders join the line of attackers who are ready to attack just behind the box.

ORGANISATION 2
The practice is 4v4 with a goalkeeper. Each team has two yellow players and two red players. If the coach calls 'number 1' the teams have to defend their opposite colour, so the two red players defend against the two opposition reds in an individual defence. If the coach calls '2' then teams have to defend against the opposite colours, so the two reds face the two opponents who are wearing yellow. The coach can continue to call 1 or 2 as the game goes on to force switching of defending.

PROGRESSIONS
- Play 3v3 in the box
- Play in a 28×20m area

COACHING POINTS
Before Phase –
- Body position to press and cover
- Read the pressure on the ball to dictate the position of the second defender
- Move with the ball and game orientation
- Communicate as a pair with voice and body shape

During Phase –
- Defensive duels
- Cover or exchange players depending on the pressure on the ball and attackers' runs
- Can defenders 'jump' on shorter distances?

After Phase –
- Recover if beaten
- Cover the 1v1 and teammate

LINKS TO FOOTBALL
All over the pitch, players press in small units. It could be the two centre backs, central midfield players or full back and winger, for example. For success, they must read triggers and cues from opponents and each other, pressing intelligently and with cover to win the ball back and deny space.

COMPACTNESS

When a team defends with compact shape they protect the middle of the court and prevent penetrative passes.

The red area of the court represents the part of the court that the team should protect with their compact shape. It is the most dangerous area an attacking team can enter. In this positioning, an opponent must play **around and** **not through** them. This enables a defence to protect the middle, control the tempo of the play, deny end product and ready themselves to counter.

Pictures

Scanning isn't just for in possession teams. Defenders should constantly scan to build 360-degree pictures of what is around them. This enables them to anticipate which markers are likely to come into their zone, as well as sniff out any danger. This is particularly important in a compact defence. Defenders should not just scan for ball carriers but also potential blockers and screeners: it is so important not to get blocked or screened in futsal!

Keeping a compact shape should be applied alongside the principles of pressing.

SESSION PLANS

The following sessions are designed to work on keeping a compact shape. Key coaching points are detailed, along with extra information to help you get the most out of each session.

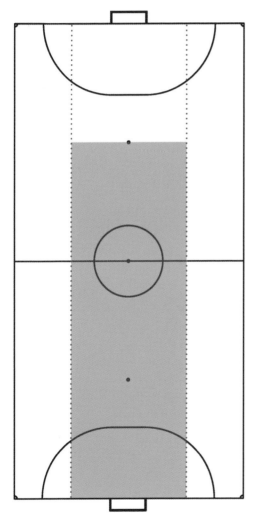

Stay compact to protect the middle of the court and force teams around and not through.

SENSE THE DANGER

FOCUS: Controlling the Court with a Zonal Defence

ORGANISATION

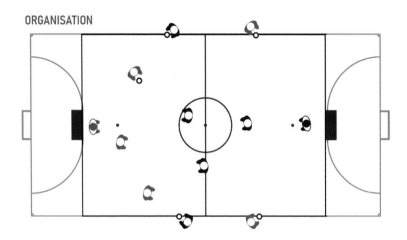

Number of Players: 10+ with 2 goalkeepers

Equipment: 2× goals, balls, bibs

IP Objectives: Combination play between three players to score.

OOP Objectives: Develop perception skills to anticipate danger by controlling a space with defensive rotations and cover.

ORGANISATION

On a shortened court (28×20m) a 3v3 game takes place. Each team has two extra players on the outside of the court in the attacking half. These players all have balls at their feet. They remain on the outside of the court until one of their teammates from inside the court dribbles outside. When this happens, the players of the in possession team on the outside become alive.

The player who dribbles the ball off the court switches with the nearest attacker on the outside. The outside player now enters the court, using their ball to attack. This movement

changes the point of the attack, meaning the defending team must sense the danger and react accordingly.

PROGRESSIONS
- Add a pivot for the players to play to
- Allow the players on the side to move up and down the side of the whole court rather than just the attacking half
- Add a floating player to help players on the inside and increase the defensive challenge
- Allow teams to score a goal by achieving a set number of passes

COACHING POINTS
Before Phase –
- Assess the direction of the possession – are opponents likely to dribble off the court?
- Sense the danger
- Perceive the pressure on the ball – can you win it back?
- Read body language and the behaviour of opponents

During Phase –
- Restore balance when the first line of defence is beaten by oncoming players
- Cover and balance in defence and positional play is important

After Phase –
- Recover quickly in straight lines to prevent goals. Defend the most threatening space
- Positive transition if the ball is won back

LINKS TO FOOTBALL

Anticipating and eliminating danger becomes more important the closer a defending team gets to their own goal. This encourages defenders to sense any danger by scanning and understanding what is likely to happen. They need to watch what their teammates do while pressing, but also look at opponents. This requires sophisticated balance and cover, reducing the risk of threatening areas.

CUT THE LINES

FOCUS: Working in Pairs when Defending

ORGANISATION

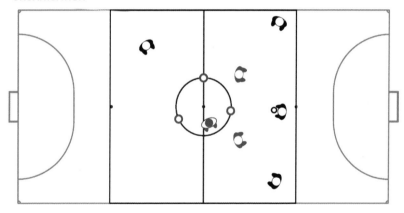

Number of Players: 6 with 1 goalkeeper

Equipment: 3x mini goals, balls, bibs, cones

IP Objectives: Use the width and length of the playing area to create scoring opportunities.

OOP Objectives: Get pressure on the ball while cutting passing lines.

ORGANISATION

The focal point of this exercise is the centre circle of the court, with the playing area measuring 20×20m. Around the outside of the centre circle, three mini goals are placed. One goalkeeper is tasked with keeping the ball out of all three.

In the playing area, two defenders attempt to prevent four attackers from scoring. Only the goalkeeper is allowed in the centre circle.

PROGRESSIONS
- If the defending team wins the ball they can break out and score in the goals at either end of the normal court
- Make it 4v3 or 5v2 depending on the age and stage of the participants and coaching priorities

COACHING POINTS
Before Phase –
- Get pressure on the ball (if distances are short enough and passing lines can be cut)
- Communication from all players including the goalkeeper
- Anticipate where the ball will be played

During Phase –
- Stop the shot and blocking as defenders and goalkeeper

- Cut off passing lines
- Stop switches of play that take out defenders
- Emergency defending if necessary

After Phase –
- React to a change of attack (if attackers decide to go for a different mini goal)
- Read the pressure on the ball in order to decide whether to press aggressively or drop off to provide cover and balance

LINKS TO FOOTBALL
This translates well to two forward players working as a pair to press the ball against a back four. Clever movements such as using body shape can make play predictable and increase the chance of winning the ball back.

Dominate with 1V1 Excellence
Every player on court should seek to dominate 1v1s and win their individual battles – whether in defence or attack. These battles are technical, physical and mental. A player should always believe that they are better and have the tools required to not only come out of a 1v1 battle on top, but to dominate that 1v1 battle. They should also use assertive, confident body language to intimidate their opponent and control the space within the defensive triangle. Following this, they need to invade their opponent's space and win the ball back to transition.

In the high press, the key 1v1 points are for a defender to stop forward play, to be aggressive by invading their opponent and to anticipate and press passing lines.

In a mid block, this requires players to get behind the line of the ball, win their 1v1 duels, track runners and dominate space.

Finally, in a low block the defender must control the space, keep their opponent in front of them (never letting them get out of sight),

Thou Shalt Not Pass

To be a top futsal player, you must be good in individual defending actions. Not only in facing up an opponent, but also in recovery runs, body orientation, positioning, controlling defensive space, defending off both sides, defensive feints, blocking and tackling. Once players can control their own defensive space they can learn to dominate and invade opposition space with a greater understanding of individual defensive skills. Coaches can improve this by getting players to consider the defensive triangle, where players analyse their position in relation to the ball and their opponent. Helping them to control and dominate space can allow them to move onto complex defensive actions such as jumping.

block shots, make quick decisions and be prepared to throw their body on the line.

In direct 1v1 battles, defenders should use triggers to their advantage. They should note

Pressing with intensity.

their opponent's weak foot and force them onto that side. If they show them away from the play and down the line they can use the sideline as an extra defender, limiting the attacker's options. If possible, they should get close enough to win the ball – ideally within an arm's length. This will also provide the physical intimidation that increases the chance of a mistake. If the defender does get beaten, they need to make a quick calculation of whether the attacker is likely to have a goal-scoring chance, how long is left in the game and how many fouls their team have committed. Remember,

fouls are currency. Teams should ideally commit five fouls per half; committing a foul to stop a goal is therefore often seen as good defending.

Defending a 1v1 successfully is one of the most celebrated actions on a futsal court.

SESSION PLANS

The following sessions are designed to work on 1v1 excellence in defence. Key coaching points are detailed, along with extra information to help you get the most out of each session.

DON'T GET YOUR WIRES CROSSED

ORGANISATION

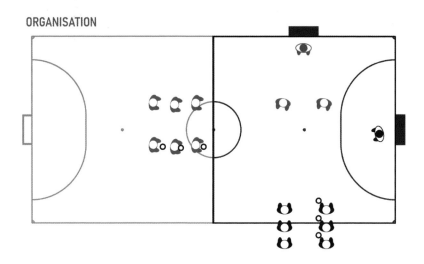

Number of Players: 8+ with 2 goalkeepers

Equipment: 2× goals, balls, bibs

IP Objectives: Score as quickly as possible.

OOP Objectives: Recover quickly and press the ball at speed.

ORGANISATION

On half a court one goal is placed in the usual position with the other placed on the sideline. Players are split into two teams (reds and blues) and then line up facing the goal they are attacking.

The session begins when the first red pair attack the goal opposite them. As soon as the action is finished – whether that's with a save, goal or the ball going out of play – the two red attackers immediately turn and become defenders. The blue pair attacks the goal opposite them with the reds attempting to recover

in time. When this action finishes, the blue attackers defend their goal and the next red pair come in to attack.

The game runs continuously – finishing only when the allotted time is up or there are no longer any balls to serve with.

PROGRESSIONS
*   Play individually
*   Play in threes
*   Alter the size of the area
*   Goalkeepers distribute the ball to attackers, allowing defenders more time to recover

COACHING POINTS
Before Phase –
*   Prioritize whether to block the pass or the shot
*   Understand when to get pressure on the ball and when to mark
*   Stay as high as possible

During Phase –
- Last line defending – blocks, tackles and attempts to win the ball back
- Force the attacker onto their weaker side
- Use the keeper as an extra defender
- Encourage the second player to get closer to the second attacker if the pressure on the ball is good enough
- Force play sideways or backwards

After Phase –
- Switch on quickly to defend against the oncoming attack

LINKS TO FOOTBALL

Few things are more exciting in football than goalmouth scrambles. Emergency defending is a necessity in many games with players forced to put their bodies on the line. This exercise improves that skill while also working on players' reactions to losing possession. In this regard it's excellent for drilling home the importance of staying focused when the team loses possession and pressing immediately rather than switching off.

DEFEND! DEFEND! DEFEND!

FOCUS: Working in Pairs when Defending

ORGANISATION

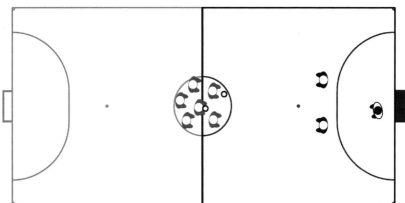

Number of Players: 6+ with 1 goalkeeper

Equipment: 2× goals, balls, bibs

IP Objectives: Score using underloads (1v1 excellence) and overloads (combination play).

OOP Objectives: Show 1v1 excellence while also working as a pair to deal with being underloaded, equal and overloaded.

ORGANISATION

A defending pair starts at the edge of the 6m area. At the halfway line a team lines up with balls ready to go.

The exercise begins with one blue attacking the two reds. Once this attack is over the blues then attack in a 2v2. The next wave is 3v2, followed by a 4v2. The coach keeps track of how many goals are scored. If the reds win the ball back they can score a goal by lobbing the ball into the empty goal at the far end of the court.

PROGRESSIONS

- Allow positive transition for the defenders so that they can score by advancing the ball up the court rather than just with a lob (in this instance the spare blue players are not able to tackle)
- Alter number of defenders to one or three depending on stage, age and coaching objective

COACHING POINTS

Before Phase –
- Assess the attackers: which is their strong foot, is one better at shooting? This helps to anticipate what is about to happen

- Apply pressure quickly
- Make play predictable
- Communicate which defender presses

During Phase –
- Cut passing lines
- Force attackers into areas where they do not want to go
- Prevent forward play
- Win the ball if possible

After Phase –
- React to the next attack
- Read the pressure on the ball to double up or press passing lines more aggressively

LINKS TO FOOTBALL

Wave after wave of attack can come when playing a superior team. This teaches players to enjoy defending and celebrate their 1v1 excellence. The practice relates well to two centre backs defending their goal in a game. Meanwhile it teaches the attackers many different attacking principles depending on the overload or underload (1v1 excellence, skills and tricks, combination play, patience).

WAVE AFTER WAVE

FOCUS: Defend Player-to-Player with Excellence

ORGANISATION

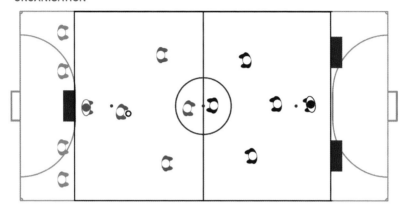

Number of Players: 12 with 2 goalkeepers

Equipment: 3× goals, balls, bibs

IP Objectives: Developing decision-making: when to shoot and when to pass.

OOP Objectives: Defend player-to-player to win the ball back and transition.

ORGANISATION

Goals are moved to the edge of the 6m area to shorten the court. Players are split into three teams of four: blues, greens and reds.

To start, the four reds attempt to score against the greens. This is complicated by the fact that the greens must defend two goals. The red team must decide when to pass and when to shoot, also assessing how to create overloads through encouraging defensive pressure and using switches of play. The greens should defend player for player, bringing out their 1v1 defending skills. With two goals to defend plenty of emergency defending can be expected.

When a shot is taken or a tackle made, the green team get possession and must now attack the other end. The red team exit the court and the blue team enter. The blues now defend. Once a shot is taken or a tackle made in this attack, the blues become the attackers and the reds re-enter the court as defenders, defending the side with two goals.

PROGRESSIONS
- Play 3v3v3 for more space and finishing
- Limit players to two touches or first-time finish

COACHING POINTS
Before Phase –
- Attacking players work as a unit with clear roles: are they going to play in a 4-0 or with a pivot, for example?
- Defending players work as a unit to manage the player-to-player defence, identifying which players to pair up to
- Body orientation of defenders to show players away from both goals

- Understand key finishing areas of second post and the top of the D and protect accordingly

During Phase –
- Prevent forward passes
- Work with support, cover and balance
- Assess where the danger is

After Phase –
- Support the next player's press
- Emergency defending

LINKS TO FOOTBALL
In this exercise the decision-making comes thick and fast, encouraging more effective decisions in front of goal on the bigger pitch and forcing players to press intelligently. It also encourages players to use different techniques to score, such as toe-pokes, laces, side-foot and clever finishes.

IN SUMMARY

Being out of possession allows a team to control the game even if they do not control the ball. By applying pressure on agreed lines, making play predictable by forcing passes and dribbles in certain directions and creating defensive overloads, a defending team can remain compact and reduce their chances of conceding dramatically. When they win the ball back, the team can then counter-attack swiftly and effectively in transition.

'Not in my half!' Press aggressively, intelligently and as a team to deny space and win the ball back in good areas.

4 TRANSITIONS

As advancements in tactical knowledge, technical skill and physical ability are made, the speed and intensity of futsal will also increase. This means that players will need to make quicker – and better – decisions on the court. When it comes to transitions, this decision-making is key.

A transition is what happens in the first few moments after a team wins the ball back or loses the ball. When this happens, teams are rarely set up for the resulting play. They are typically disorganised, which can often lead to underloads or overloads. This is because when it happens, the transition is unexpected.

To gain a competitive advantage, teams and coaches can plan to exploit weaknesses in opponents, then capitalize on these weaknesses with effective transitions. In a sport where one goal can make all the difference, the importance of these moments cannot be overstated.

PICK YOUR MOMENT

When it comes to coaching transition, there are two areas to focus on:

Positive Transition: Transition from defence to attack after winning the ball back from an opponent.
Negative Transition: Transition from attack to defence after losing the ball to the opponent.

In the very first moments of a transition, there are likely to be gaps in the defending team's set-up. This means that in the modern game, many teams are actually at their most vulnerable when **they** have the ball. This is why it is so important for teams to have stability behind the ball in attack.

The best players know when and where to move when possession changes. Their

Transitions: make them count.

individual actions and decisions help to decide the result of the transition for their team. These are qualities that can seem innate, but they are in fact learned. This is because futsal provides constant feedback and learning opportunities that develop players.

For me, futsal players deal much better in transitions than football players. With the smaller court, fewer players and quicker ball speed, every action in futsal is magnified. Every consequence is greater. The feedback is instant and occasionally brutal. If a player chooses not to track their player in transition, for example, it could easily result in a goal against. This underlines the importance of making good, quick decisions, and is just one of the countless reasons as to why futsal is such an effective tool for developing world-class footballers around the globe.

When coaching transitions, there are three different decision-making elements to focus on: individual players, small groups of players, whole team situations. These all need to fit within an overall strategy that links in with your coaching philosophy. Importantly, players need to be given the tools to understand transitions while also being trusted to execute any action with full autonomy.

POSITIVE TRANSITIONS

There are three different phases when it comes to positive transitions. The first is the **opening phase**. This is where the player in possession must think forward and look forward so that they can play forward. This player, who is the first to receive the ball in the transition, acts quickly, ideally with forward momentum.

Positive transition actions can go sideways or backwards. However, analysis shows that these going sideways or backwards significantly reduce the chance of success in gaining territory or scoring a goal. When the ball goes backwards or sideways, it gives the opposing team vital seconds in which to recover and regroup. Coaches should therefore encourage a positive, forward action in the first phase of a positive transition. This could be a forward dribble, a drive forward or a pass.

Following this first action, a team enters the second phase of a positive transition: **the progression phase**. Here, a team must progress the attack, usually by moving the ball into the central axis of the court.

Having the ball centrally opens up more passing lines, providing more options for the

Transitions are a great opportunity to attack a disorganised defence.

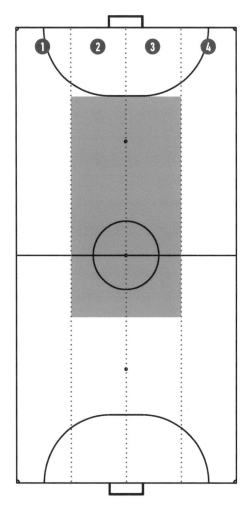

The progressive phase is the first phase of a positive transition, typically taking place in a team's defensive third.

abandon. They will not be able to regroup as a defensive structure until they have evened out the overload. This is one of the reasons that it is best if the attacker attempts to engage a defender before passing or shooting. Having two attackers running beyond the ball to offer forward, penetrative passing options will emphasize this and provide greater options for the ball carrier.

Top Transition Tip

Overload is better than speed!

Moving the ball centrally also increases stability for the attacking team. If the team does lose possession in this phase, resulting in a negative transition, then they are better set up to recover and regroup quickly. Here, they should be looking to attack as a 3v2, for example, rather than 4v2, as this will maintain cover.

A positive transition is concluded in the **finalizing phase**, which is where the final action takes place. Typically, this is a shot at goal. It is ideal for the attacking team to target the weak side of the defending team before shooting. They should shoot centrally 10–12m from goal if their opponents do not engage them. When doing so, it is important that the shooter strikes the ball hard, high and across the goalkeeper. This increases the chances of 'finishing the action'. Ideally, there will also be an attacking runner to the back post to increase the likelihood of success. If executed well, the action will finish with a goal. If not, then shooting in such a manner reduces the goalkeeper's chances of catching the ball and launching a counter-attack.

In this phase the attacking team should be encouraged to take risks. They should always be looking to score.

player in possession and giving the team greater control. It allows for better and more efficient runs off the ball, both in terms of overlapping and underlapping on either side. The defending team is unable to use the sidelines as extra defenders, meaning that it is more challenging for them to direct the attacking team into an area where it is likely that they can win the ball back.

When the team progresses with an overload it will unbalance the opposition's defence, which must eventually decide which attacker to

IN SUMMARY

1. Think forward, look forward, play forward.
2. Move the ball centrally.
3. Finish the action.

NEGATIVE TRANSITIONS

When you control negative transitions, you control the game. This is the same in all invasion games and a common trend among the top teams. Having a stable defensive set-up not only reduces the risk of conceding goals, but also allows your players to be more confident in possession and take more risks.

Players must understand the key perception skills, decision-making skills, and tactical actions that are needed in a negative transition. These include:

- Anticipation
- Pitch geography
- State of the game
- When and where to perform actions
- When, where and how to press
- When to block passing lines

As with positive transitions, a negative transition can be broken down into three distinct phases: deny and deflect, delay, emergency defending.

The first phase, **deny and deflect**, requires players to attempt to win the ball back as early as possible. This means applying fast pressure on the ball to stop the opposition from starting their positive transition and organising an attack.

It is known as the 'gegenpress' in football. If the team cannot win the ball back then they should aim to stop their opponent's forward momentum or deflect the attack away from the centre of the court. This will limit the attacking team's options and control of the situation, making it tougher for them to move into the progression phase while also allowing defensive teammates time to recover their positions.

If a team is unable to apply pressure on the ball in the first instance, it is best not to engage and move into the second phase of negative transition: **delaying**.

Here, the defending team should delay their opponents and deny them from passing forwards. They can do this by blocking passing lines and denying the space available to counter-attack in. Defenders should recover quickly in straight lines, getting back behind the line of the ball with trajectory toward the top of the D and the back post. The aim of this is to delay the attack and create balance to prevent the defensive team from being outnumbered.

Controlling the centre of the court is key to success. Whichever team has dominance in lanes 2 and 3 is most likely to have a positive outcome. Once the middle has been managed by the defending team, it is important to then stop passing lines and push opponents onto their weaker attacking foot, as well as toward

Work together to deny space and deflect away from goal.

one side of the court. This needs to be tactically executed within seconds.

Use the Court

Remember: the touchline is an extra defender. Using it effectively can help regain possession and minimize overloads.

If the attacking team manages to get to the 10m line or move the ball wide again in a dangerous area, then the defending team moves into the final phase of the negative transition: **emergency defending**.

Ultimately, this phase comes down to blocking shots and preventing shots centrally. Here the goalkeeper should be used as the ultimate defender. Extra bodies can be put on the line to limit the opponent's ability to score.

The goalkeeper's role in negative transition is hugely important. In the first phase they will defend their half, followed by their D and then, in the final phase, their goal. They therefore start as a sweeper keeper, which is also why many of the best football goalkeepers in the world play high up the pitch.

The goalkeeper provides an extra advantage to the defending team. If the ball is played wide by the attacking team to the weak side of the defensive unit then the defending team is likely to be outnumbered. Here the goalkeeper can be employed as an extra defender to provide defensive balance. It is their job to press the ball, while the opposite defender takes up a more zonal position on the back post to provide damage limitation.

If the ball is played wide to the strong side of the defensive unit, however, and the team is not outnumbered then it is important that defenders lock on and stay player for player until the end of the phase, while also providing cover for the second post. In this scenario, the goalkeeper stays to protect their goal.

IN SUMMARY

1. Apply pressure on the ball quickly to win it back as early as possible.
2. If unsuccessful, deflect the attack away from the centre of the court.

Up close and personal... anything to stop the counter!

3. Deny the opponents options while teammates recover in straight lines.
4. Push opponents onto their weak foot, toward the strong area of the defensive unit.
5. Block the shot.

Ultimately, having principles and concepts of negative transitions can limit damage in dangerous areas. Having a collective and individual plan that you train and teach can make your players' actions instinctive, aiding their execution of the perceptual, decision and action phases.

The following sessions work on transitions for your team. When delivering these sessions, observing how your players react to a turnover of possession can be useful. The following points cover key areas to assess in negative transition:

- When the attacking team lose the ball, do all the players make an attempt to return to a defensive shape behind the ball?
- Do they make recovery runs that shut down space and provide cover and support to their teammates?
- Depending on the style of play, do the players immediately near to the ball move to win it back? If not, what do they do?

SIT DOWN

FOCUS: Improve Decision-Making in Positive Transition with Numerical Advantage

ORGANISATION

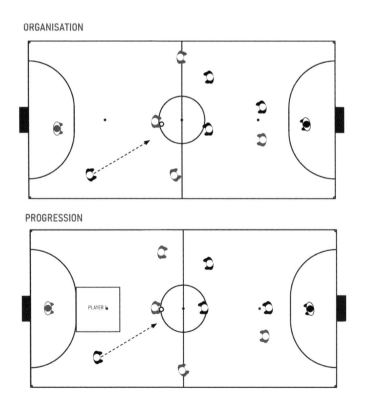

PROGRESSION

Number of Players: 10 (8 + 2 goalkeepers)

Equipment: 2× goals, balls, bibs

PT Objectives: To improve decisions in overloaded transitional positions in order to finish with quality and at speed.

NT Objectives: To develop principles of deflect, deny and cover when outnumbered.

ORGANISATION

On a full court of 40×20m, a 3v3 game takes place with two goalkeepers. The game takes place as normal but when possession is lost, the player who touches the ball last either through a turnover of possession or an unsuccessful shot must sit down in the position that they touched it until the ball has crossed the halfway line once more. This gives the attacking team a 4v3 advantage for a short period of time.

PROGRESSIONS

- The player sits down and can then get straight back up to shorten the advantage time for the attackers
- Limit time to counter once an attacking team has passed the halfway line to six seconds
- The coach controls the seated player and when they can return to the game
- The opposition goalkeeper can call which player must sit down at any point in the game

COACHING POINTS
Before Phase –
- See the forward pass early if it is on

During Phase –
- Keep the ball central in lanes 2 and 3
- Overload is better than speed – prioritize quality of movement
- Look for speed and accuracy when moving the ball into the attacking third

After Phase –
- Provide stability in attack with adequate cover
- Make support-to-score runs toward the second post and top of D
- Look at recovery runs (straight lines to get back behind the ball)

LINKS TO FOOTBALL
Transition in controlling the centre of the pitch is so important in both football and futsal. Finishing over the goal line in positive transition makes sure a team does not get their counter-attack countered, and also helps teams to maintain attacking stability. It also emphasizes that if a player 'sells' themselves in football by diving into a challenge with a speed of approach that is too quick and subsequently beaten, they risk creating a moment of negative transition that puts their team at risk.

NEED FOR SPEED

FOCUS: Improve Decision-Making in Positive and Negative Transition

ORGANISATION

PROGRESSION

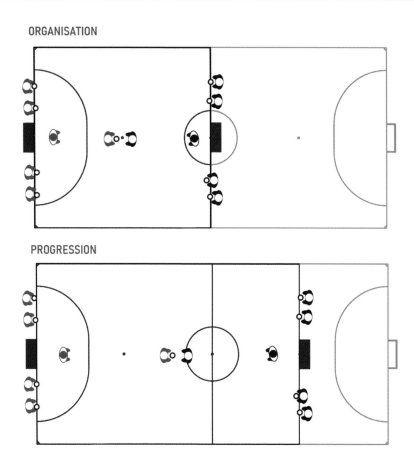

Number of Players: 10 (8+2 goalkeepers)

Equipment: 2× goals, balls, bibs

PT Objectives: Attack with speed to create overloads when a shot or action is finished.

NT Objectives: Delay attacks when underloaded while teammates make quick recovery runs.

ORGANISATION

The practice begins with a 1v1 in the middle of the playing area. After the first action is finished and the ball is no longer on court – whether that's a shot or goal or the ball being kicked off court – another player joins the one now in possession to make a 2v1. If the ball remains on court after the action is finished, then the second player does not join in. For example, if the red player shoots and it misses the goal, a second blue player drives in to attack that red player in a 2v1. After the blues have shot, a second red player joins the attack. It is now a 2v2, with the blue player who took the shot acting as a recovering defender. The next attack is a 3v2 in the blues' advantage. The play continues progressing in this manner until it becomes a full 5v5 with goalkeepers. Once that action is over, the game has finished and resets.

PROGRESSIONS
- Make the pitch longer
- Change the entry point of the players on the pitch
- Allow two players to enter the pitch at once but only one ball

COACHING POINTS
Before Phase –
- Be ready to attack at speed
- Scan for the space to attack before entering the pitch

During Phase –
- Attack the space
- Rapid speed
- Travel with the ball or pass forward quickly if possible
- Finish the action over the goal line

After Phase –
- Recover quickly to defend

LINKS TO FOOTBALL
As football increases in speed and intensity, players cannot just stop and admire the action they have just performed. Instead they must be alert to the next action, never switching off so that they can suitably support the next play or recover in negative or positive transition. In futsal the next action is the most important; this is also increasingly the case in football.

3V3 TO 2V2

FOCUS: Improve Decision-Making in Positive Transition with Numerical Advantage

ORGANISATION

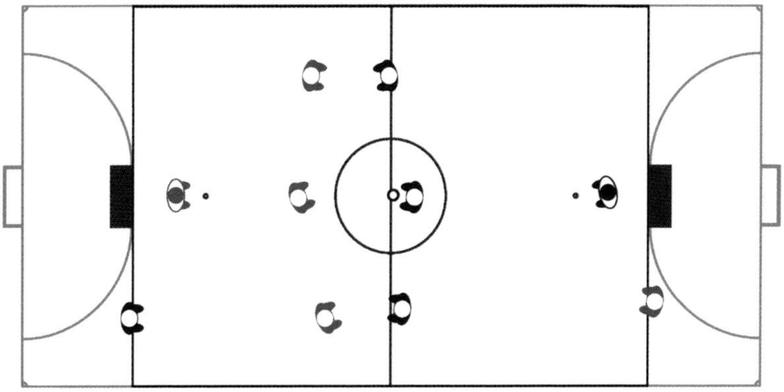

Number of Players: 10 (8+2 goalkeepers)

Equipment: 2× goals, balls, bibs

PT Objectives: To improve decisions in overloaded transitional positions in order to finish with quality and at speed.

NT Objectives: Positioning to cut passing lines, keeping opponent and ball in sight at all times.

ORGANISATION

On a court of full-width and reduced length (both goals are placed on the edge of the D) a 3v3 game begins. If a player misses the target or has their shot saved, they must swap with one of their teammates who is waiting next to the goal. This teammate may only enter the action after the player who took the shot reaches the goal line and high-fives them, creating a moment of 2v3 transition.

PROGRESSIONS

- Change on loss of possession, not just shot
- Play the same game as a 4v4 on a full court
- Play the same game as a 2v2

COACHING POINTS

Before Phase –
- Attack with height and width
- Finish or attack centrally as the ball carrier

During Phase –
- Be fast in the first action
- Control the centre of the court

After Phase –
- Maintain stability in attack
- Block the centre
- Control the central axis

LINKS TO FOOTBALL

Transition in controlling the centre of the pitch is so important in both football and futsal. Transitions happen quickly, meaning the importance of every decision is magnified. With eleven players, footballers have to constantly play with overloads and underloads. Punishing opponents who are underloaded is important in gaining territory and exploiting space to shoot at goal.

GET TO THE HALF

FOCUS: Improve Decision-Making in Positive and Negative Transition

ORGANISATION

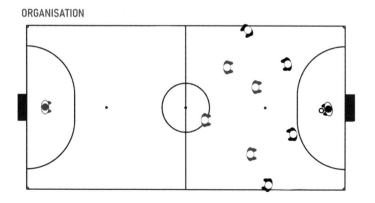

111

Number of Players: 10 (8+2 goalkeepers)

Equipment: 2× goals, balls, bibs

PT Objectives: See positive transition opportunities and take advantage with good decisions.

NT Objectives: Press aggressively to prevent opponents from getting to the halfway line.

ORGANISATION

On a full court two teams play against each other with normal numbers. The game always begins with a goalkeeper restart. The attacking team must then work together to dribble the ball over the halfway line. Once they manage this, they are allowed to attack either goal. This will create lots of transitions.

If the ball goes out of play then play is restarted from the goalkeeper of whichever team should have possession. If a team scores then the opponent gets possession.

PROGRESSIONS

* Make the halfway line higher – perhaps three-quarters up – to incorporate building and combination play
* Reduce the size of the playing area, even to a half court, and play as a 3v3 or 4v4. This will increase the number of quick finishing opportunities

COACHING POINTS

Before Phase –

* Press the ball and passing lines
* Movement to create space from the attacking team

During Phase –

* Positivity in possession (face forward, combination play, don't stop the ball)
* Accelerations and changes of direction to sense overload opportunities
* Stop forward passes if defending
* Slow down and delay in negative transition when defending

After Phase –

* Sense the danger if the point of attack changes
* Recovery runs
* React in transition to support the ball carrier in the correct way

LINKS TO FOOTBALL

Transitions happen rapidly. If just one player switches off it becomes a huge disadvantage. This reinforces the need for all players to take responsibility. On the smaller court with fewer players every decision is magnified. The feedback is brutal. This teaches footballers they must stay alert always – a game can change within seconds. Especially when they are all involved in every action.

MAXIMIZE THE OVERLOAD – MARC CARMONA

FOCUS: Improving Positive Transitions

Marc Carmona is the most successful FC Barcelona Head Coach to date, and moved to become a coach educator for FCB and a futsal pundit after many years of success. Here he shares four session plans to work on positive transitions.

ORGANISATION

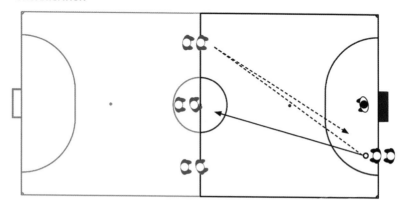

PROGRESSION

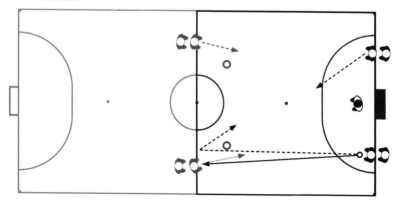

Number of Players: 10+2 goalkeepers

Equipment: Goal, balls, bibs

PT Objectives: Make the right pass with the right timing after engaging the defender.

NT Objectives: Control the centre of the court while outnumbered.

ORGANISATION

Players are split into two teams: red and blue. Reds set up on the halfway line in waves of three as the attacking team. The blues set up next to the goalpost and are defending.

The blues begin the exercise by passing to a red attacker, who plays it back to the blue. The blue then selects which of the three attackers to play it to. As soon as the blue plays this pass they defend the goal while the three attackers attempt to score.

PROGRESSION

- The reds set up in waves of two attackers. The blues also have two defenders, with waves set up at the side of each goalpost. The game begins with the same sequence. However, the second blue defender is now a recovering defender and must run around one of the red cones by the halfway line after playing the pass to the reds. This blue defender is not allowed to join their teammate in defence until this run has been made. This encourages the red team to finish their attack quickly, before the situation becomes a 2v2.

COACHING POINTS
Before Phase –
- Attack the space and ball to transition quickly

During Phase –
- Be fast in the first action
- Lock the defender in order to allow an overload run
- Timing and weight of the pass to stop the defender recovering and the goalkeeper from smothering

After Phase –
- Movement after passing – either get on the ball again with a supporting angle or get onto the back post for a second post finish
- Finish the action and conclude the attack

LINKS TO FOOTBALL
Transition in controlling the centre of the pitch is so important in both football and futsal. Engaging defenders with your first touch is key in tight areas such as in and around the box.

ENGAGE, THEN EXPLOIT – MARC CARMONA

FOCUS: Improving Positive Transitions

ORGANISATION

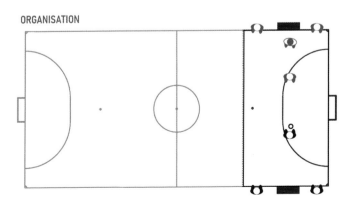

Number of Players: 6+ (and 2 goalkeepers)

Equipment: 2× goals, balls, bibs

PT Objectives: Make the right pass with the right timing after engaging the defender.

NT Objectives: Control the centre of the court while outnumbered.

ORGANISATION

In a long but narrow playing area, two players start in the middle. These two players attempt to score against a goalkeeper. As soon as the final touch comes and the action is finished, the next two players come and attack in the opposite direction, against the other goal. The two players who have just attacked must now attempt to recover and defend their goal. This is likely to be a 1v2 until the player that took the shot gets back in to defend. Once this action is over, the defenders exit the court, the two attackers become defenders and two new attackers enter the court. This is a physically demanding game, with three minutes being the ideal block to work for.

PROGRESSION

- The last player to touch the ball must touch the goalpost or high-five the goalkeeper before they are allowed back onto the court to defend

COACHING POINTS

Before Phase –

- Attack the space and ball to transition quickly

During Phase –

- Be fast in the first action
- Lock the defender in order to allow an overload run
- Timing and weight of the pass to stop the defender recovering and the goalkeeper from smothering

After Phase –

- Movement after passing – either get on the ball again with a supporting angle or get onto the back post for a second post finish

LINKS TO FOOTBALL

It isn't just in futsal where the advantage of a counter-attack can last for only a matter of seconds. This exercise teaches players to make the most of their advantage and finish quickly but effectively to prevent defenders from recovering.

DOMINATE THE HALF – MARC CARMONA

FOCUS: Improving Positive Transitions

ORGANISATION

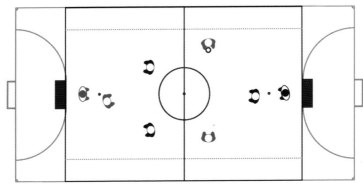

Number of Players: 6+ (and 2 goalkeepers)

Equipment: 2× goals, balls, bibs

PT Objectives: Make the right pass with the right timing after engaging the defender.

NT Objectives: Control your half by blocking the passing line and limiting the available space.

ORGANISATION
In a shortened court of 28×16m, a game takes place between three blues and three reds. Each team has one defender and two attackers. These defenders must stay in their half throughout the game. This leaves a constant 2v1 in the attacking halves. When the ball enters the attacking half, the action must be finished within fifteen seconds.

PROGRESSIONS
- Attackers must finish the action within ten seconds
- Make it a 2v2 in each half with one attacker allowed to cross into the other half
- Make it a 3v2 with a recovering defender from the other half

COACHING POINTS
Before Phase –
- Attack the space
- Attack the ball

During Phase –
- Be fast in the first action
- Positive touches
- Lock the defender in order to allow an overload run
- Timing and weight of the pass to stop the defender recovering and the goalkeeper from smothering

After Phase –
- Movement after passing – either get on the ball again with a supporting angle or get onto the back post for a second post finish

LINKS TO FOOTBALL
This exercise is fantastic for paired movements, which happen all over the football and futsal pitches. It can even be done within a section of an eleven-a-side pitch to help vertical or horizontal units.

STAY AND PLAY – MARC CARMONA

FOCUS: Improving Positive Transitions

ORGANISATION

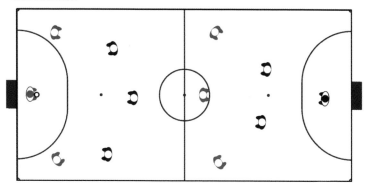

Number of Players: 10+ (and 2 goalkeepers)

Equipment: 2× goals, balls, bibs

PT Objectives: Make the right pass with the right timing after engaging the defender.

NT Objectives: Control half the court when defending outnumbered.

ORGANISATION
A normal game takes place. However, each team has two defenders and three attackers. These players must stay in their designated halves and must not cross into the other half. This creates constant 3v2 situations. Attacks should have finished actions within fifteen seconds.

PROGRESSIONS
- If a player can dribble from the defensive half to the attacking half then their team is allowed to attack as a 4v2
- If a player crosses with a dribble, a recovery defender is also allowed to enter
- After these two progressions, a team can reset by placing a different player into the half. This encourages rotations

COACHING POINTS
Before Phase –
- Attack the space
- Attack the ball

During Phase –
- Be fast in the first action
- Positive touches
- Lock the defender in order to allow an overload run
- Timing and weight of the pass to stop the defender recovering and the goalkeeper from smothering

After Phase –
- Movement after passing – either get on the ball again with a supporting angle or get onto the back post for a second post finish

LINKS TO FOOTBALL
Reading triggers is an important skill to anticipate what is about to happen and to take advantage of any given situation. Positioning this exercise in two × 18yd boxes would create plenty of finishing opportunities and emergency defending.

GET BACK! – MIGUEL RODRIGO

FOCUS: Transitions

ORGANISATION

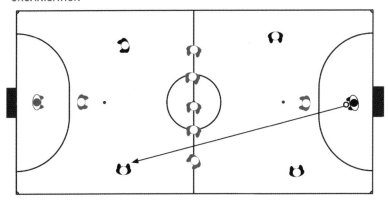

Number of Players: 10+ (and 2 goalkeepers)

Equipment: 2× goals, balls, bibs

PT Objectives: Combine at speed to finish.

NT Objectives: Delay until support arrives with the recovery defender.

ORGANISATION
Two attackers set up in each half. They are joined by one defender, with all other defenders lining up on the halfway line.

The practice begins when a goalkeeper throws the ball to an attacker in the opposite half. This should be done with quality and at appropriate speed. This is because the goalkeeper is the first line of the attack and often the first chance a team has to create (particularly if the keeper has just caught the ball). As soon as the attacker takes their first touch, one defender is allowed to recover from the halfway line. The attackers must progress the ball quickly, keeping the 2v1 advantage for as long as possible until the recovering defender makes it a 2v2.

Once the action is over, the first defender returns to the halfway line while the recovering defender stays in the half. The other goalkeeper then distributes a ball into the opposite half for the next pair to go 2v1 with one more defender recovering from the halfway line. This continues in waves.

PROGRESSIONS
- Play 3v2 with a recovering defender
- If the attackers don't score then they change places with the two defenders (hold bibs to make this easier)
- Play in waves to encourage keepers to distribute quickly and attackers to finish the action to minimize the risk of their counter-attack being countered

COACHING POINTS
Before Phase –
- Create space to receive ball from the attacker
- Recovering defender should anticipate where the danger is going to be

During Phase –
- Quality of keeper's distribution
- Positive first touch facing forward
- Immediately engage the defender
- Vertical and horizontal runs
- Defender should delay by shutting off the passing line

After Phase –
- Recover back to position

LINKS TO FOOTBALL

Counter-attacks happen regularly in football, as do overloads and underloads. This teaches players to maximize overloads and to reduce the disadvantage of being underloaded by delaying the opponent.

FINISH THE RONDO

FOCUS: Maximize the Counter-Attack

ORGANISATION

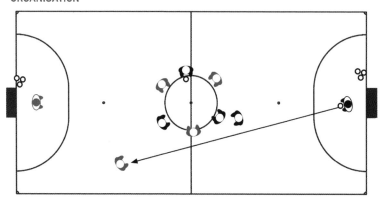

Number of Players: 6+ (and 2 goalkeepers)

Equipment: 2× goals, balls, bibs

PT Objectives: Finish the attack.

NT Objectives: Quick recovery runs.

ORGANISATION

Six or more players take part in a rondo around the centre circle. They number themselves 1–6 (or up to however many players are taking part). One or two players defend in the middle of the rondo depending on the ability of the players.

At random intervals, the goalkeeper will call out a number from 1–6. That number must immediately drop out of the rondo and attempt to score. It is up to that player where they receive the ball from the goalkeeper (one goalkeeper distributes while the other stops shots).

To progress the game, once one goalkeeper calls the number of an attacker, the opposite goalkeeper can call out another number. This second number now becomes a recovering defender.

After this action, both players return to the rondo, which continues.

PROGRESSION

- Increase the amount of numbers called – it could be a 2v2 or 3v3 for example

COACHING POINTS

Before Phase –

- Be prepared to attack
- Open body position to finish quickly

During Phase –

- Use different types of finishes
- Positive touches
- Travel with the ball at speed

After Phase –

- Recover back to the middle quickly – the longer the player takes the less likely the in possession team is to keep the ball in the rondo

LINKS TO FOOTBALL

This mimics third player runs from deep coming onto the ball to finish quickly before defenders have the chance to react.

DEAL WITH THE TRANSITION – MICO MARTIC

FOCUS: Defensive Transition

Mico Martic has enjoyed a long and successful career as a futsal player and coach. Having most recently coached the Finnish national team at the UEFA Futsal Euros, he is credited with transforming futsal in Finland since starting with the national team in 2013. He has also coached Croatia. Prior to his coaching career, he represented Yugoslavia as a player before captaining the Croatian national team. Here, he shares a session to work on transitions.

ORGANISATION

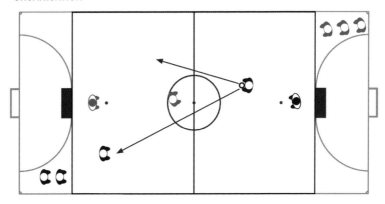

PROGRESSION

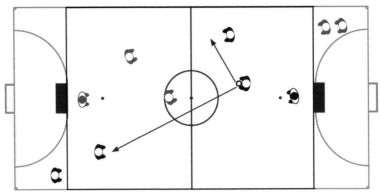

Number of Players: 10+ (and 2 goalkeepers)

Equipment: 2× goals, balls, bibs

PT Objectives: Improve accuracy and finishing in offensive movements when overloaded.

NT Objectives: Develop the understanding of defensive positioning and when to engage the attacker.

ORGANISATION

The game takes place in a 28×20m area on a shortened court. The goalkeeper starts with the ball and passes to their attacker. As soon as this happens, the attacking team's pivot is allowed to step onto the court. This creates a 2v1.

When the attack finishes, the game resets in the other direction. The defending team now attack the other goal, with one of their pivots entering to create a 2v1. The last attacker to touch the ball must run to make an exchange with a teammate to bring in another defender.

PROGRESSIONS
- Allow the goalkeeper to pass direct to the pivot on the ground
- Allow the goalkeeper to pass to the pivot directly in any way
- Start with a 2v2 to make a 3v2
- Start with a 3v3 to make a 4v3

- Reduce the time allowed for the attack to increase the intensity

COACHING POINTS
Before Phase –
- Work hard to get pressure on the ball to stop passing angles to the pivot
- Control and dominate the space in the 1v1

During Phase –
- Stop forward runs with the ball
- Prevent passes into the pivot
- Tackle or intercept

After Phase –
- Communicate with the goalkeeper if the ball does go into the pivot – who goes to the ball and who stops the pass to the back post?
- React quickly in positive transition

LINKS TO FOOTBALL
This exercise links well to two centre backs or central midfielders learning to defend central areas. They must work in pairs to shut off forward passing lines while then advancing to press the ball, sniffing out dangerous attacks and minimizing the overload.

5 SPECIAL PLAYS

One of the key points of differentiation between futsal and football is the use and impact of special plays. In this chapter, we'll cover a play unique to futsal – the powerplay – and one which has a far greater impact in the small-sided game: 4v3.

THE POWERPLAY

The powerplay is when the goalkeeper comes out of their goal and plays as a fifth outfielder. This strategy is high risk, as the goal is left untended, but also has high reward due to the overload created in the attacking half.

Once the keeper has touched the ball once in their own half, they are not allowed to touch it again unless they are in the opponent's half. This means that when using the powerplay tactic, a team's goalkeeper will typically roll the ball out to their teammates before either sprinting up the court into the attacking half or substituting with an outfielder player who then also runs into the attacking half before receiving the ball.

Ideally, the keeper will remain on court and act as the fifth attacker. This means that if the attack breaks down, they will be confident in racing back and resuming activity as a goalkeeper. On the occasions when the attack breaks down and an outfield player has taken over from a goalkeeper, they must be comfortable returning to the goal or substitute quickly with the actual goalkeeper without putting their team at risk of conceding a goal.

Not all goalkeepers are confident using their feet out on court. How you decide to utilize the powerplay tactic should relate back to your coaching DNA. Are you looking to develop players, or is your primary aim to win? Are you looking to teach players risk and reward, or would you rather play it safe?

Although on the face of it such a strategy seems attacking, it can also be used to maintain a lead and run down the clock while keeping possession. Using five outfield players to keep possession against four defenders opens up passing lines and puts the defending team under pressure to win the ball back quickly. Such a time to use the tactic could be when the attacking team has conceded five fouls in the half and does not wish to concede a sixth (giving away a 10m penalty in the process), and therefore wants to run down the clock.

Often, however, the tactic is used when a team is chasing a game.

Whichever team deals best with the overload will be the team that scores the most goals. For the attacking team, they must use the overload to always keep at least two passing lines open and to constantly move the defence, tiring them out in the process. In possession principles remain in place here: by moving the ball at speed, showing control and patience, and finishing the action, a team can improve their chances of scoring more than the opponent.

Seizing the Chance

If the **opportunity to go direct** emerges, the attacking team should seize it. This could even be before they have established their offensive set-up. If the opponent is disorganised, the attackers have to capitalize.

If the opponent manages to organise themselves, the attacking team should position themselves across the four lanes, with **players carefully selected based on their**

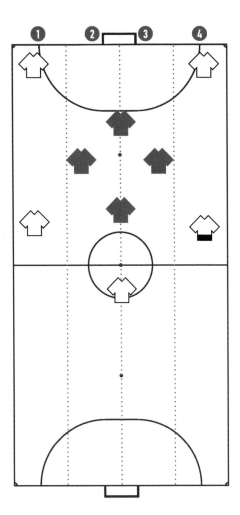

The white team is attacking using the powerplay tactic. They are positioned to make the court as big as possible, giving them plenty of space. There is room for flexibility within this set-up, such as the two wingers moving onto the border of the middle and wide lanes so that they engage their defender. The player furthest back acts as a safe pass, dropping deep into their own half if necessary to retain possession (this cannot be done by the goalkeeper, who can only receive the ball once in their own half). This becomes especially important if the defending team applies aggressive pressure. As the ball moves from side to side, the two players furthest forward also move laterally. One opens up a passing line vertically, while the other moves toward the back post for a tap-in. As the ball moves back across the court, their roles reverse.

strengths. The best passer of the ball should be the one set up in the middle as they dictate the play with their passes. The best back post finishers should be positioned highest. If there is a player with a particularly strong shot, they should be on the wing. Left-footed players should be on the right-hand side, while right-footed players should be on the left-hand side. This is because it is easier for players to use their strong foot to play the ball across the court. It is also quicker for the ball to reach them on their strong foot when positioned in this manner. They are able to receive the ball on their safe side, which provides implications for defenders regarding how aggressively they are pressed and increases the likelihood of ball retention.

If they are pressed aggressively then they can use their body to protect the ball, allowing them to keep playing with their **strong foot**, orienting their control as they look across the court for options. Maintaining possession with their strong foot then allows for opportunities to more easily disguise touches or passes. On a more offensive basis, playing inverted aids the false pivot system with players more easily able to hold the ball up using their strong foot.

The attacking team should use the powerplay to **build pressure**. High ball speed constantly disorganises the defence, increasing the amount of space that can be exploited. There should never be a need to dribble. Such play slows the game down and gives the defending team a chance to press as a unit. Of course, players can dribble, but that essentially turns the 5v4 into a 1v1: which of those situations will have the biggest impact on the attack? The answer will likely depend on your coaching philosophy.

The game is best slowed down only in order to entice a defender in before exploiting the space they have left with a quick switch of play. Effective circulation of possession furthers the ability to build pressure. After a few circulations, **player movement** – such as the wingers threatening the next passing lanes and engaging the defenders – can imbalance the defence. All this ultimately increases a team's chances of being able to shoot in and around 10m from goal.

Such player movement can create overloads. It is ideal to create these overloads on the weaker side of the defence. In wide areas, the opportunities to go 2v1 are more common, and have the added benefit of potentially drawing the covering defender positioned at the base of the defence – usually the best defender of the team – out of position. Teams should then attack space in and around the defensive lines and complete actions at the back post and top of the D.

Top Tip

Due to the 5v4 overload, 1v1 attacking actions here should perhaps not be adventurous – utilize the extra player! A 1v1 minimizes the overload and allows the defence to become matched up.

Defending the Powerplay

For the defending team, however, they must turn the underload into an advantage. Using compact shape, they can ensure that they are played around rather than through. When the ball goes into high areas, they can then smother the ball and block passing lines. Using body positioning, they can make play predictable, forcing it in one direction (ideally to the weakest player on court). Any triggers, such as slow play, should be pounced on. If the defending team manages to win the ball back, it only takes one positive touch before they can get a clear, free shot at their opponent's goal. This compactness, along with clever positioning such as using the touchline as an extra defender, can negate the overload and match up numbers between the defence and attack.

The starting point for a defending team in the powerplay scenario should be deep – preferably at the top of the defensive third. This minimizes the space for the attackers to play in, but is not so deep that it is easy for them

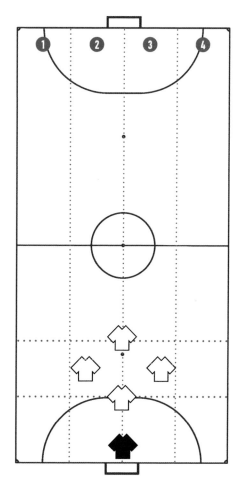

The Diamond Defence against the powerplay.

to get shots off at goal. The highest player should comfortably be in their own half and ready to engage just as an opponent shoots (around 10–15m from goal, on defensive lines 4 or 5). It is their job to make play predictable. Although the main priority for every defender is to be played around rather than through, if the highest player can shut off one side of the court with their body positioning then it makes it easier for the other defenders to anticipate what is about to happen.

The initial set-up mirrors a **diamond**. This is if the ball is in a central area. When the ball moves into a wide area, the defensive set-up mirrors a **box**, rather than a diamond. Essentially, a team goes from 1-2-1 to 2-2, with the fix moving behind the winger that engages the ball. The pivot then positions themselves to stop the pass across the court, with the furthest winger dropping back to stop the attacker playing a diagonal pass to the back post. The defensive shape might then further change depending if an attacking player is in the middle of the defensive structure. In this scenario, the emphasis will be on stopping central passes. Defences will more likely line up in a 2-2 to achieve this.

If the opportunity arises, the defending team should **prepare to disrupt** their opponent's set-up. Similarly to the attacking team, the defenders should position players within the set-up based on their strong foot – and their strengths. Those players within the squad that are most defensively solid should be those selected to defend the powerplay, while a right-footed player should be positioned on the left and vice versa. This means that if a diagonal pass is intercepted – which is often the case – they can shoot quicker, and also first time, with more confidence.

The defending team should apply enough pressure to **stop unnecessary shots**. They should mark their territory clearly and press the opponents if they dare to venture into that territory. As with the compact team shape principle of out of possession play, they should close the middle of the court. Maintaining a **zonal shape** will help to do this and is important given the overload. As soon as a trigger is given, the cue is there to press.

No matter how good the defence, there will be times when they become overloaded. In these situations, the defenders need to manage the space and not the players as best they can by ensuring appropriate cover and balance on their underloaded side. If necessary, they must be prepared to perform emergency defending at the back post and the top of the D, throwing themselves in the way of dangerous shots.

There may be times when the defence can force a 1v1, 2v2 or even 3v3 situation. When this happens, getting pressure on the ball can force an opponent backwards or even result in a mistake that allows for the ball to be won. These are key moments to look out for as a team; the defensive triggers will be the same as the normal defensive triggers in terms of decisions for when to press.

4v3

Following a red card, a team must play with one player less. Unlike in football, however, this is not permanent. After a spell of two minutes or when the team concedes a goal, they are allowed to bring a player back and resume with four outfielders. Given that this advantage is only for a short period of time, the attacking team must make the most of it.

The basic concepts mirror that of the powerplay.

The four attacking players work to make the court as big as possible, positioning themselves across the four lanes to open up forward passing lines and create opportunities to penetrate with shots. As with the powerplay, there should never be a need to go 1v1. High ball speed, attacking in and around defensive lines and overloading the weak side of defence all help to increase the chance of success.

Given the fewer players on the pitch, a red card is noticed far more in futsal than it is in football. The two-minute deadline for a player coming back on court also adds excitement and can unnerve an attacking team if the defence remains resolute. When it comes to defending the 3v4, the same concepts are once again in place that were there for defending the powerplay. Rather than a 1-2-1, a team sets up in a 2-1 (many also choose to go 1-2). This reinforces stability at the back while the player at the top attempts to make the overload redundant by making play predictable. The court should be made as small as possible with such positioning.

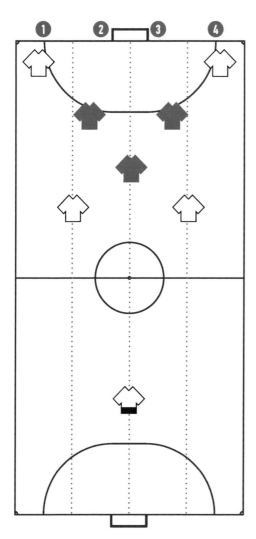

Typical set-ups in a 4v3 situation.

When playing with an overload, always look to work opportunities to get shots at goal.

If possible, pressure should be applied on the ball – especially if the attacking team gets within shooting range (within 10m of the goal). Plenty of emergency defending can be expected in a 3v4 situation, requiring brave defenders. Often coaches select three players fresh from the bench. This helps a team to deal with the physical demands of being under-loaded for up to two minutes.

SESSION PLANS

The following sessions are designed to work on attacking in 4v3s and defending in 3v4s. Key coaching points are detailed, along with extra information to help you get the most out of each session.

OUTNUMBERED

FOCUS: Improve Defending Skills of Pressing, Covering, Floating and Using Peripheral Vision While Outnumbered

ORGANISATION

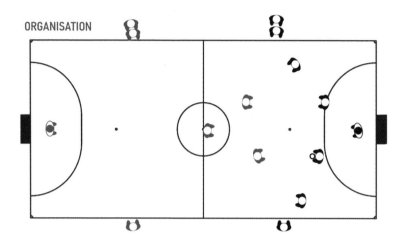

Number of Players: 14 (12+2 goalkeepers)

Equipment: 2× goals, balls, bibs

IP Objectives: The attacking team must try to play quickly and combine as a group in order to make three passes before they can cross the halfway line.

OOP Objectives: To develop principles of denying forward play, defending on multiple lines and trying to prevent the overload.

ORGANISATION

In a full court (40×20m) a 4v3 game with two goalkeepers takes place. The attacking team has to make three passes before they can cross the halfway line. The attacking team is always allowed to play with four players, creating an overload against the defending team. The defending team must press to stop the attacking team from getting over the halfway line. If unsuccessful, and the attacking team does make it over the halfway line, then they are free to score. When retreating into their own half, the defending team should be encouraged to now defend as if they have had a man sent off in a 3v4 low block.

When an attacking player loses possession of the ball they must leave the court while their team defends. When the defending team wins the ball back, they are able to gain an extra player throughout their attack – making the overload now 4v3 in their favour. They must also first play three passes in their own half before they are allowed to cross the halfway line.

PROGRESSIONS

- Use as a warm-up with more players (5v6 or 6v7, for example)
- The attacking team needs to make five passes before they can cross the halfway line
- The attacking team must score with a first-time finish
- To work on transitions, the player that loses the ball is allowed back in to defend

with their team once they have run to the opposite goal and high-fived the keeper

COACHING POINTS
Before Phase –
• Defenders stop forward passes and control the space, making the court as small as possible

During Phase –
• Recognize the opportunity to win the ball when matched up
• Defend passing lines
• Floating and spatial awareness as a defender to provide cover and balance
• Invade space and win the ball back as a unit

After Phase –
• Resetting the press if beaten
• Work as a unit in the first or second line press, forcing play in one direction to make it predictable
• Positive transition from defence to attack

LINKS TO FOOTBALL
This practice teaches responsibility to forwards, encouraging them to understand why it is important to prevent forward passes, press the ball and block passing lines, along with how to win the ball back with numerical balance. As football develops, forwards are expected to press from the front, with tactics such as counter pressing growing in importance. Forwards are the first line of any team's defence.

OUTNUMBERED 2

FOCUS: Improve Defending Skills of Pressing, Covering, Floating and Using Peripheral Vision While Outnumbered

ORGANISATION

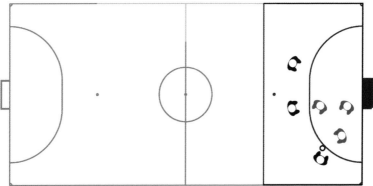

PROGRESSION

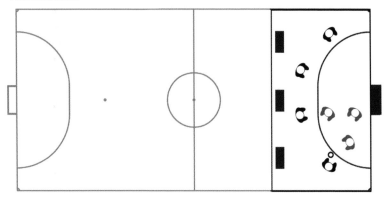

Number of Players: 7

Equipment: Goal, balls, bibs

IP Objectives: The attacking team must try to play quickly and combine as a group in order to find gaps to play through and score.

OOP Objectives: To develop principles of denying forward play, defending on multiple lines and trying to prevent the overload.

ORGANISATION
Around a standard-size futsal area, four attacking players have possession and must try to score through three defending players. The three defenders aren't initially allowed to leave their designated area while the attacking team isn't able to enter the area. They can, however, pass through it.

The defending team must attempt to stop the attacking team from scoring by rotating, pressing the ball as much as possible, and offering cover and balance behind. There is no goalkeeper to protect the ball, meaning the defenders must work intelligently and aggressively.

The defending team has ten balls to defend. The coach keeps the score. After these ten balls, the teams switch over with the defenders becoming the attackers.

PROGRESSIONS
* Incorporate mini goals for the defenders to shoot into if they win the ball
* The attacking team can enter the area to put more pressure on defenders
* Allow the defending team to have a goalkeeper to protect the goal.
* Increase the defensive zone to increase the challenge

COACHING POINTS
Before Phase –
* Defenders stop passes to the fourth player and cut out passing lines
* Anticipate and notice where the player is passing to (assess their body shape and in particular their hips)

During Phase –
* Recognize the opportunity to win the ball when matched up
* Defend passing lines
* Floating and spatial awareness as a defender to provide cover and balance

After Phase –
- Rest the press if beaten
- Cover quickly if the ball gets switched to the other side

LINKS TO FOOTBALL

Underloads happen all over the pitch. By adding in a goal, this adds an element of danger. It especially mimics emergency defending with players encouraged to work intelligently to minimize the underload and block off passing lines with body shape, key elements to learn when defending.

IN SUMMARY

Special plays are enhanced chances to score a goal. Being able to play with an overload allows in possession principles, such as looking forward to play forward, to emerge more easily. With the powerplay commonly used by teams – and constantly evolving – it is essential that teams feel comfortable in possession and also out of possession with its use. Essentially, it will all come down to risk versus reward.

Which team will want it more?

6 SET-PLAYS

Set-plays are of critical importance in the game of futsal. Every corner is an opportunity to get a shot at goal. Every free-kick a chance to score. Every sideline the ability to exploit space and create. Every keeper restart is able to beat the pressure and create overloads. No wonder that such a high percentage of goals come from set-plays. At the highest level,

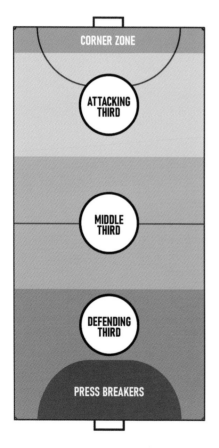

The places on the court where different set-plays take place. These influence the type of kick-in, for example, that is taken.

effective set-plays are very often the difference between victory and defeat.

Once a team gets into the attacking third all set-plays should be performed with the aim of getting a shot at goal. Once the referee blows their whistle, there is a countdown of four seconds until the set-play is turned over to the other team. Four seconds is a long period of time, certainly long enough to disrupt an opponent and create space in their zone. To enhance the chances of scoring, techniques such as direct and indirect blocks, checks, false movements and creativity are required. For maximum effect, the set-play taker should allow these runs and movements to take place and for opportunities to develop by using the four seconds as currency. Stay patient, stay alert and trust teammates to create passing lines and unbalance a defence before the four seconds are up.

At the top level very few successful set-plays are spontaneous. Most elite teams have numerous corner, free-kick, sideline and keeper restart routines, but with multiple outcomes depending on what actions the defenders take. These will typically be named or numbered and repeated regularly in training until they become second nature. Every player should know exactly where to move for each set-play regardless of the position they find themselves in on court. **Planning**, then, is the ultimate power behind successful set-plays.

Set-pieces are a chance to utilize the entire squad. With up to fourteen players available, just five are needed to execute a set-play successfully. Coaches can change an entire team just for the set-play – particularly if it is a free-kick. Alternatively, they can choose just one player to bring on, for example one that is

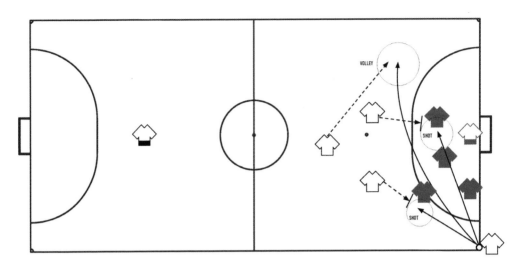

Example Set-Play Routine: Volleyed Corner. Three attackers set up in a horizontal line on the 10m line. The marked circular area is where the corner taker aims to pass the ball. It is vital that this area is off centre. This is because if the pass is intercepted, it is harder to execute a successful counter-attack from a wide area. On the taker's call, the nearest attacker to the ball begins to slowly move toward the grey area. The other two attackers block the deepest two defenders to prevent them from getting to the grey area. When performed correctly, this allows the shooter a free shot at goal. The taker's pass should be 'stabbed' rather than scooped so that it is flat – again, to make it harder to counter, but also to put pace on the ball for an easier finish. After this, the taker should run to the back post for a second post finish from the volley.

an excellent finisher. This then effectively gives them the role of the kicker, similar to American Football.

Player Roles

For any set-play, there are six different positions with different skills required.

Goalkeeper:
- Good distribution with the feet
- Decoy position to keep defence guessing
- Control the attack/offer support behind the attack

Taker:
- Making and executing a planned decision to create a goal-scoring opportunity
- Clever enough to make decisions based on defensive actions (if a defender escapes the press, perhaps the pass is better to go to the blocker rather than the intended recipient, for example, as the presser will now unexpectedly be free)
- Patient enough to use all four seconds

Blocker:
- Good ownership and spatial awareness
- Discrete
- Clever timing, ensuring the defender has no chance to escape the block and to open up the required passing line at the last moment
- Selfless
- Feels negative transition well

First Contact/Opposite Winger:
- Ability to play forward
- Can play first time with quality
- High knowledge of set-plays

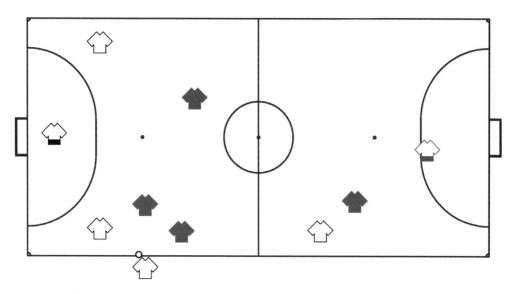

Kick-in example. The fix sets up close to the taker. Meanwhile, the other winger provides width and the pivot provides depth. The taker rolls the ball to the fix, then runs inside the court and blocks the nearest attacker. This buys the fix time on the ball to make their decision. Their first option is to play a pass down the line to the pivot – ideally, the movement of the taker will have created the space to do this. If that pass is not on, the switch across the court to the other winger is a possibility. If this happens, the taker can continue their run into the centre of the court to create a 2v1 on the far wing. If the defender is too close to the winger then the diagonal pass into space for the winger to run onto could be on. Alternatively, if the block is good, the fix can travel with the ball into the centre of the court. This will create more opportunities for passes. Finally, if the defensive pressure is good then the goalkeeper provides a safe option, allowing the attackers to reset in formation.

A high ratio of goals come from set-pieces – do not undervalue them!

Shooter:
- Strong shot to finish the attack with their first touch
- Understands the second outcome well

Finisher/Pivot:
- The 'fox in the box'
- Sniffs out second balls, anticipating what is about to happen
- Clever mover
- Lands often in the middle of the D or on the back post

The best surprises are the best planned. False movements and disguises may surprise the defending team, but really they're the result of frequent practice. These creative moments may be planned for the entire team or just an individual. Regardless, each set-play solution should have multiple outcomes based on how the defence reacts (how many players are in the wall, how many on the goal line, how many marking?). Every single player must know every single set-play.

It is the job of the attacking team to create disorganisation in the defence. Having multiple outcomes leads to confusion, making it harder for the defensive team to guess what is about to happen. For example, if a defender escapes the block, the blocker may now be free to receive a pass and shoot at goal. If the blocker manages to successfully block the defender just half a second before the kick is taken, an opportunity for another attacker should now have arisen to shoot at goal.

Top Tip

Wrong-footing opponents to take advantage of the moment is key. Double movements create uncertainty, allowing attackers to gain a split second against a defender.

It's important not to overload youth players or novices. Instead of coaching them all multiple outcomes at once, start with just one outcome.

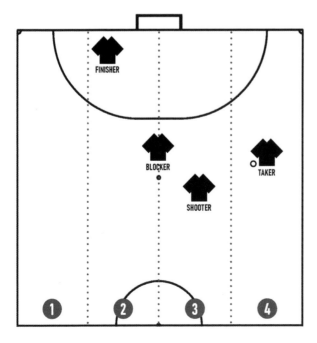

The player roles at set-plays, illustrated within the attacking third.

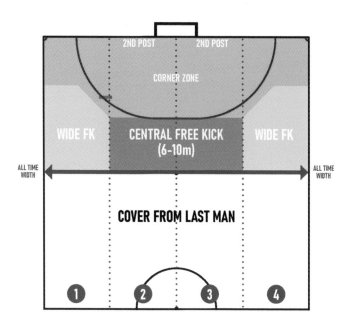

The location of different set-plays within the attacking third. Note the importance of cover from the last player in case of a negative transition.

Once that has been learned, a second outcome can be introduced and then a third. Those who are more experienced will be better equipped to deal with multiple outcomes all at once.

The most experienced high-level coaches will have a great deal of set-pieces to hand. They will have corners, kick-ins, restarts and press breakers that work against zonal defences, player for player defences and mixed defences. This is also the case in football, where the best coaches will work out which set-piece to use depending on the opponent's defence. What is crucial in futsal is that players block and screen to open up passing lines, exploit spaces and gaps, and create time for the shooters; space is at a premium.

Press Breakers

Not all set-plays are in the attacking third. If the attacking team is being pressed from a keeper restart, they have the chance to perform 'press breakers', where their choreographed movement can open up space to play forward and receive the ball in dangerous areas, breaking through the opponent's press. If successful, this may even result in the defending team no longer pressing from restarts. This can be done within the possession stage of game models, or drawn out separately. The initial set-up can be used interchangeably with a 3-1. Press breakers can be seen as an in possession moment or a set-play moment, depending on you as a coach and your game model.

Principles of Set-Plays

Once the set-play has been decided, it requires high-quality execution from all players on court. Movements should act as guidelines. Though they are important to do in synchronized timing, if a defender does something unexpected – such as escaping the press or not tracking their opponent – then the taker should choose a different outcome to the one agreed. Much of the onus on set-plays is on the taker, who must always **read and react to** the defensive actions by watching the opposition. If the opponent defends well and there is no option on, the taker can simply shoot and create chaos in the D.

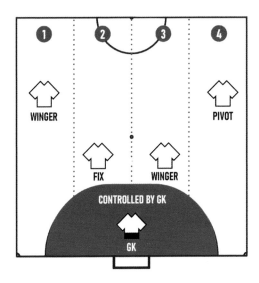

A typical set-up from a press breaker.

Top Tip

Don't just teach players actions: teach them to watch the opposition so that they can improve their perception skills. A player's action should depend on what the opposition does.

When the taker plays forward or switches play they must do so with quality. Screeners and blockers help to open passing lines. Given the success of such techniques in futsal, football set-plays are beginning to use discrete blockers. In futsal, players are allowed to block so long as they do so without pushing. Rather than directly pushing into a player, the blocker

PRESS BREAKER

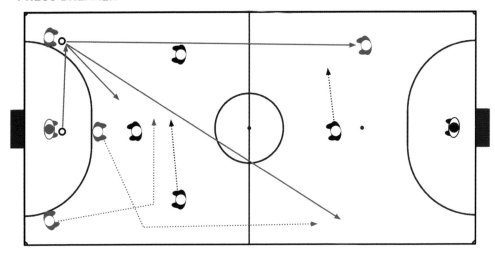

Press Breaker example. The in possession team sets up in a 3-1 in this basic press breaker. The goalkeeper holds the ball in their left hand to indicate they will play it to the left player. Once they have rolled the ball, the movements begin. The pivot moves to the same side as the ball to open up a passing option down the line and create space on the other side of the court that can be exploited by the fix's movement. The opposite winger moves centrally to create a triangle with the player in possession and the pivot. They can receive a pass to then play into the pivot, bounce a pass back to the passer or turn into space. This movement can also create space for the fix by drawing the opposition winger into a central area. The fix pulls out wide, into the space vacated by the winger that moves centrally. They can then receive the ball deep. Or, if the space is there (and given the movement of the pivot, it likely will be there), they can run forward to receive a diagonal pass. It is down to the player who receives the pass from the keeper to decide the best option. This will be based on the reaction of the opponents' defenders.

should stand firmly, blocking the path of the defender without using their arms.

The attacking team should have a commitment to penetrate and score with each set-play. Players should first and foremost be a threat, whether they are making a decoy run, blocking, shooting or passing. At least one player should attack space in behind and get in the D, while the player that shoots should do so with a first-time finish. This not only gives the defending team less time to react, but also helps to build mental pressure on the defenders.

DEFENDING SET-PLAYS

To defend set-plays effectively, teams must have a plan of how to limit space as a unit. The primary purpose of the defending team is to protect the goal, as is illustrated in the typical set-up of defending a corner.

When defending set-plays in the defensive third it is the goalkeeper's job to set up their team and position them accordingly. This is because the goalkeeper can see all of the action in front of them. When the ball is played by the attacking team, players must make a commitment to defend 1v1 and as an individual. The player that they are marking cannot be allowed to score. This is the first phase of defending the set-play.

The second phase is much more aggressive. If the shot is poor or the ball is intercepted, the defending team can swiftly transition with a counter-attack, making the most of the disorganisation in their opponents.

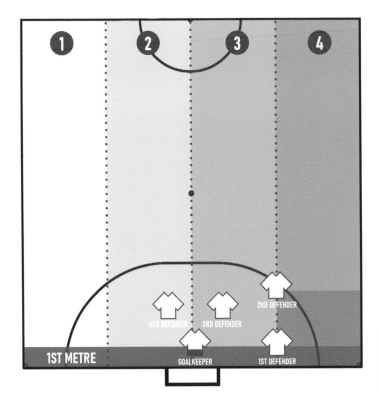

How to defend a corner effectively. This mirrors a high press turned on its side, with three lines of defence to provide cover.

Each player has a key role when defending set-plays.

Goalkeeper:
- World class shot-stopper
- Controls the team
- Takes the first metre on the corners to stop any balls across goal

First Defender:
- Usually an attacking player
- Takes the second metre
- Screens the ball into the danger area

Second Defender:
- Usually the pivot
- Can get out quickly
- Clever to not get blocked

Third Defender:
- Best positional defender
- Strong and can sense danger
- Gets out quickly to stop shots

Fourth Defender:
- Strong defender
- Does not get blocked
- Can get out quickly
- Covers shots by blocking the back post

When coaching set-plays it is really important to coach body shape and perception skills. This allows players to anticipate any screens and blocks coming as early as possible. If this does happen, players should work as a team to overcome them. Players should not move until the ball moves, each controlling their own space.

SESSION PLANS

The following sessions are designed to work on set-plays. Key coaching points are detailed, along with extra information to help you get the most out of each session.

FOUR SECONDS TO SAVE THE WORLD

FOCUS: Finishing in Restarts

ORGANISATION

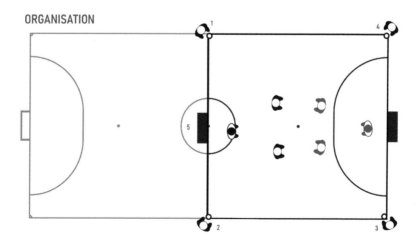

Number of Players: 10 (8+2 goalkeepers)

Equipment: 2× goals, balls, bibs

IP Objectives: Work as a pair to finish on goal.

OOP Objectives: Work as a pair to prevent shots at goal.

ORGANISATION

In half a court, two reds and two blues set up in the middle. There is a goal either end with four servers (one in each corner). These servers are numbered from 1–4 with the goalkeeper being number 5. Numbers 1 and 2 provide kick-ins, 3 and 4 give corners while 5 is a goalkeeper restart.

The coach calls the numbers in order. This is important. If the numbers are made random then there is a chance it'll become a finishing exercise rather than a restarts exercise. After the call comes, the taker has four seconds to take their restart – just as in a game. Once the action is over, the coach should give the players time to reset, once again placing the emphasis on the restart rather than on finishing.

To make the exercise high risk, if the attacking pair do not hit the target from the restart then they must exit the playing area and a new attacking pair come in. If they score then the exercise resets and the first server takes their restart again. However, if the defenders win the ball and then score in the opposite goal, they become the attackers and the attacking team go in to defend.

PROGRESSIONS

* Give each team a set number of balls to play with, for example, how many can they score from ten restarts? This adds a competitive element between the teams

COACHING POINTS

Before Phase –
* Movement as a pair to create the space
* Decide which player strikes (do they have a dominant foot/stronger strike?)
* Should one player block or screen for the other?
* Fix players

During Phase –
* Recognize defensive pressure
* Can you escape the block?
* If the defenders cheat can you punish them?
* Encourage servers to make the most of the four seconds – wait for the right moment
* Make as few passes as possible – ideally just the one from the server
* Finish first time if possible
* Finish the action

After Phase –
* Support the player shooting
* Get to the second post for a back post finish or to get rebounds and deflections
* Stop negative transitions

LINKS TO FOOTBALL

Football is increasingly looking to other sports for set-piece routines. As a result, blocks at set-pieces are becoming more common. They are seen as an effective way to create space that often escapes the attention of the officials. This teaches players how one small block or movement across a defender can open up space for a shot. These basic building blocks can be applied to both defensive and offensive situations in football.

GOOD AS THREE, BETTER AS TWO

FOCUS: Finishing in Corners

ORGANISATION

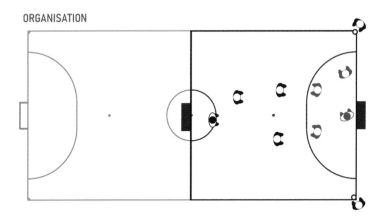

Number of Players: 9 (7+2 goalkeepers)

Equipment: 2× goals, balls, bibs

IP Objectives: Work as a pair to finish on goal.

OOP Objectives: Work as a pair to prevent shots at goal.

ORGANISATION

The practice starts with a corner kick. The blues attack first with two nominated attackers out of the three attempting to score from the corner. The taker has four seconds from the coach's call to play the ball. If the blues score then they get to take another corner. If they don't score in the first phase and the red team get the ball under control then the third players become alive and make the game 3v3 in the second phase. Alternatively, if the blues don't score in the first phase but the reds do not get possession then the blues can decide whether to carry on playing 2v2 or to unlock the third players.

  If the reds win the ball and transition to score in the goal on the halfway line then they will become the attackers.

PROGRESSIONS
* Make the pitch longer
* Add kick-ins once the pitch is longer

COACHING POINTS
Before Phase –
* Movement as a pair to create the space
* Utilize blocks and screens
* Double movements

During Phase –
* Finish first time
* Take on a role and commit to it: blocker, screener, shooter, taker

After Phase –
* React to the second phase
* Defend the transition
* Rotate again to maintain possession

LINKS TO FOOTBALL
Finding half a yard to finish can be the difference between winning and losing. This exercise teaches good habits of finishing quickly, which encourages strikers to shoot before the keeper is set. It also shows the importance of carefully planned out set-pieces.

LEAVE, GET OUT

ORGANISATION

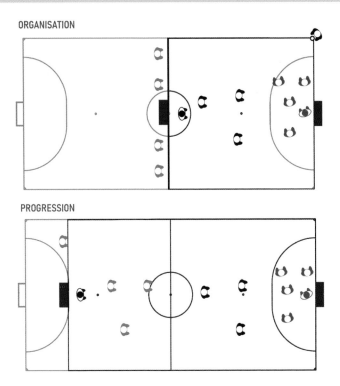

PROGRESSION

Number of Players: 12 (4v4+4 with 2 goalkeepers)

Equipment: 2× goals, balls, bibs

IP Objectives: Work as a team to score set-plays.

OOP Objectives: Stay solid in the first and second phases when defending corners.

ORGANISATION

Four blues attack against four reds, starting off with a corner. The coach gives them ten corners in a row and sees how many they can score. If the defending team kick the ball out during any corner then the coach puts a second ball anywhere on the court to give the attackers a second phase of attack. If they score at any point

then the number of corners they are given resets to ten.

The only ways for the defending team to get out of defence are to successfully defend all ten corners or to win the ball and score in the goal on the halfway line. If they do manage to get out then they are rewarded with a rest on the sidelines while the team that was attacking become the defenders and the team that was resting go in to attack.

PROGRESSIONS

- If the defending team win the ball then they break out by dribbling over the halfway and transitioning to an attack of 4v3. This three is made up from the team resting. The team that took the corner is not allowed to recover to the defensive half

141

COACHING POINTS

Before Phase –

- Defensive principles of body shape to see runners and blockers
- Stay strong and solid
- Understand defensive role (zonal, exchange or player-to-player)
- See the danger
- Be on your toes to stay alert
- Slight movements left and right to put off taker and put doubt in their mind

During Phase –

- Don't get blocked

- Recover the ball and transition
- Defend in the first and second phase
- Communication

After Phase –

- React to the second phase
- Defend the transition
- Finish in transition

LINKS TO FOOTBALL

Reinforces the defensive set-play principles of zonal, player-to-player and mixed while also working on staying organised in the second phase attacks.

BARCA (PRESS BREAKER)

FOCUS: Set Moves to Get out of Pressure in Restarts from the Keeper

PHASE ONE

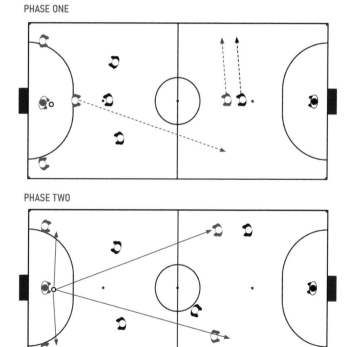

PHASE TWO

Number of Players: 8+2 goalkeepers

Equipment: 2× goals, balls, bibs

IP Objectives: Gain court supremacy and secure the ball or progress possession.

OOP Objectives: Press aggressively to deny passing lines while providing cover.

ORGANISATION

The goalkeeper always starts with the ball. This is a choreographed move where all players work in unison to give the goalkeeper multiple options for their throw. The two deepest players drop low just outside the box and face forward so that they are ready to receive a pass. The middle attacking player drives and runs through on the opposite side to the pivot. The goalkeeper's decision should then be made based on what the opposition does. Do they follow runners, for example, or exchange? Different responses will have different solutions. Each repetition must take place within four seconds.

PROGRESSIONS

- Alternate the player who runs into the space opposite the pivot to create uncertainty in the defence and limit their ability to read the movement
- Introduce blocking and screening to create more problems (rather than running through, the middle attacking player can block the first defender, allowing the player who receives the first pass to drive freely through the court to open up passing lines)

COACHING POINTS

Before Phase –

- Understand where each player's starting position is, allowing appropriate height and width to make the court big
- Welcome pressure from the opponents to create more space in behind

During Phase –

- Use the four seconds to your advantage so movements and defender reactions can play out
- Create multiple options by synchronizing movements
- The quality and timing of the goalkeeper's delivery will dictate the success of the play
- Outfielders must look to play forward or secure possession depending on the pass

After Phase –

- Movement to support the ball carrier in a fast attack, ensuring one player covers while three attack

LINKS TO FOOTBALL

Most top-level teams have moves in order to break pressure. The use of the goalkeeper as a key decision-maker to break the press is hugely important, particularly when opponents press high. This allows teams to play out from the back successfully. Having such set movements gives players confidence when being pressed, as they understand it is possible to use that pressure to create opportunities in high areas up the pitch.

7 GOALKEEPING – ANDREW READING

The foundations of all great modern teams are built from the goalkeeper. Protected by just four teammates, the futsal goalkeeper often finds themselves in the thick of the action.

A keeper can expect to be placed under far more pressure than in the eleven-a-side game. There'll be more saves, more touches of the ball, more distribution, more organisation, communication, leadership, a greater number of decisions to make with less time to make them.

A good keeper gives a team confidence. A keeper with a flaw, however, may put the team at risk. At the elite level, opponents can spot flaws quickly and then create a gameplan to exploit those flaws.

To succeed, a keeper must remain calm and focused on the task at hand. They should be agile and flexible: some of the best saving techniques in futsal require unnatural body positions. Shot-stopping should be instinctive and quick. They should be willing to stop dangerous attacks and start their own. Courage out of possession and bravery in possession are essential, while the ability to analyse plays and make effective tactical plans can be the difference between a good and great keeper.

The following pages discuss the essential requirements in detail, while sharing exercises to help develop those technical and tactical skills.

EXPERT GUIDANCE

For this chapter, we've called on the help of specialist goalkeeping coach Andrew Reading. The former England futsal and beach soccer national team keeper became the first Englishman to play professional futsal abroad when he signed for Odorheiu Secuiesc Futsal

The best keepers are leaders.

Club in Romania. Following a successful playing career, Andrew went on to work as a goalkeeper coach for the England national futsal team, New Zealand national team and in the United Arab Emirates Premier League, amongst others.

IN POSSESSION

Distribution

The futsal keeper does far more than just stop shots. In many ways they're futsal's version of a quarterback, initiating attacks from deep and creating chances for outfield players. To do this, they need to be comfortable playing passes with their feet and their hands.

When distributing, a keeper's main task is to make sure that the player they are passing to can control the ball instantly. If the player has to waste a touch getting the ball under control then the opponents are more likely to be able to press them and shut down the space they have available.

There are three main ways to distribute with the hands:

The Roll
For an effective roll, the keeper should keep their body weight low to the ground. Their knees should be flexed, the lead leg in front of the body and bent, while the arm action should go straight through. It is vital that the ball maintains full contact with the surface and rolls at the appropriate speed: too slow and it may be intercepted, too quick and it may be hard for the receiver to control. The more the ball bobbles when rolled, the less likely it is to be cleanly controlled. For an elite level roll, keepers should play the ball in the direction the receiver needs to be facing (forward if under no pressure, toward their own goal if under pressure).

The 'Swazz'
While the roll is primarily for shorter distances, the 'swazz' is for medium to longer distances –

often around the halfway line and beyond. The ball is thrown from a slightly higher angle, though the body shape is still low. In fact, the more flex in the legs the better. The arm action is nice and low – not quite as much as in a roll – and then comes through quickly. The ball then rolls along the court smoothly.

Spear Throw
The spear throw is needed for distribution of longer distances. This differs from the more rounded, bowling-style action used for throwing longer distances in eleven-a-side. Here, the spear throw is used because it adds an element of disguise. This is especially important as opponents attempt to read what is about to happen and apply pressure accordingly. To perform the throw, the keeper should flex their legs to give a stable foundation. A good guideline for the height of release is the position of the intended target. For example, if the keeper wishes to hit the chest of the pivot, they should release the throw from the height of their own chest. This will help to ensure a flat throw that travels with speed. Speed is key to reduce the reaction time of defenders.

Throw Low

By keeping the body shape nice and low, when the ball is released it reduces the chances of it bouncing around. The higher the ball comes out of the hand, the more likely it is to bounce and skid because of the angle it leaves the hand. If the player is receiving the ball under pressure (particularly likely for a pivot), then it becomes harder for them to play with.

Distribution begins from the moment the ball is out of play. As the keeper walks to retrieve the ball, they should do so while facing play. This gives them a vital chance to assess the tactical information, which will then inform which kind of throw they should use.

- Are the opponents pressing or is a trap being set?
- Where are your teammates and their opponents?
- Which passing lines are open?

Once the information has been gathered and the ball has been retrieved, the keeper can then use the space of the D to their advantage. By moving around they can create different angles and new passing lines.

When the ball is in their possession, the keeper has four seconds until they must release it (this is also the case if the keeper catches the ball from open play, rather than retrieving it from outside the court to restart play). Rather than see these four seconds as a limit, instead they should be reframed as an opportunity. Four seconds is a long time, and once movements and rotations start it can change the pictures in front of the keeper greatly. Coaches should emphasize patience. Keepers should hold their nerve and allow the time for movements to occur fully and spaces to be exploited. They must not only trust their teammates, but also trust themselves to deliver.

Granted, a futsal keeper must analyse a lot of information in just four seconds. At no point does an eleven-a-side goalkeeper have to work under such time constraints or pressure!

So much of a goalkeeper's distribution in futsal is about disrupting opponents. In a typical game the keeper can expect to throw the ball countless times. Each throw is an opportunity to create an attack. It could be a throw into space for a teammate to run onto, a direct throw to the pivot or a traditional press-breaker. These can be co-ordinated with hand signals, communication or pre-choreographed movements. However, if the keeper continues to throw in exactly the same manner, opponents will begin to anticipate what is about to happen, which will then allow them to apply more pressure. This is why it is particularly important for a keeper to use their entire area to create new passing lines, and also to

feint movements and add disguise to their throws. This freedom of expression should be encouraged: the more creative the better! Adaptability and creativity are key.

Fast Hands, Fast Feet

A keeper who is comfortable with their feet essentially adds a fifth attacker to a team that is in possession. Given that there are only four outfield players, this means that a keeper's teammates will always have a passing option available if they know that the keeper is comfortable to play with their feet (unless they have already touched the ball in their own half, in which case the keeper must make the decision to stay in their half where they cannot receive the ball again or fly to create a passing option). Playing back to the keeper is a great option if a team is being put under pressure. Because it creates an overload it often reduces pressure. If the opponents decide to press the keeper, that then opens up a spare teammate and new offensive opportunities.

This trend has begun to take shape in football, too. Players such as Manchester City's Ederson have changed the way the game is played. Being so comfortable with his feet means that Ederson can take part in possessions of his team, which then draws in pressure from the opponent. This creates space behind the pressure. Because Ederson is so adept at both short and long passing, he can then exploit this space.

Ederson, just like a futsal keeper, is a creator who can provide continuity of play and help teams to build from the back. It is no coincidence that Ederson's background is in futsal.

To help their teammates as much as possible in possession, the keeper should:

- Create a passing line or outlet for their teammates
- Tell their teammates which foot they'd like to receive the ball with
- Look at the ball and court while maintaining peripheral vision

- Receive the ball with the sole of their foot and take a first touch which allows them to play a pass with their second touch
- Change the approach or angle of their hips to play if necessary
- Consider where their teammates should receive the ball

These considerations must all be made alongside the tactical information taken on board before receiving the pass:

- Which areas can the keeper take advantage of?
- What openings are the opponents allowing to be exploited (for example, are they player-to-player marking or zonal? Are they flattened out, bringing the ball over the top into play, or do they have multiple lines of defence?)
- Are the opponents pressing in sync?
- Is the counter-attack on? If not, are the opponents dangerous on the counter?

When the ball is at the keeper's feet, they also have just four seconds with which to play. That means it is important they analyse the tactical information available to them quickly and efficiently so they can make a good decision. The more experience they have doing this, the better their decisions will become – and the more instinctive.

Create Chaos

The best way to emphasize specific goalkeeper techniques is to create chaos in training situations. By adding physical and mental pressure to a keeper and increasing the speed and frequency of decisions they must make, training can become harder than a match. This means that when a keeper comes to play in a match, their decisions are more instinctive and they find it easier than the training sessions they usually take part in.

However, the four-second rule does not apply to a goalkeeper if they receive possession in the opponent's half. When a keeper is comfortable with the ball at their feet, they can play as a fifth outfielder at any point in the match. Indeed, from kick-ins the keeper can offer a passing option as a 'fly keeper' to create an overload higher up the pitch, then drive forward into the opponent's half. This can also be the case on the counter-attack. If a keeper catches the ball they can elect to dribble forward into the opponent's half to create an effective overload.

A goalkeeper with a powerful, accurate shot provides another desirable option for a team. It is always important for the action to be finished in a counter-attack, but this is even more the case if it is the keeper who shoots. A weak shot that is straight into the hands of the opposition keeper can lead to a dangerous counter-attack – particularly because keepers can score with a kick from their hands if they catch the ball.

A goalkeeper's shot should therefore be powerful. If the shot comes from the organised position of the powerplay, there are further factors that come into play. Should they shoot to the second post, for example? Perhaps it's best to keep possession rather than shoot, or maybe they should even move into a central attacking area to compromise defenders?

As can be seen, the keeper is far more than a stopper...

Mentality

There's a well-known saying that you don't have to be crazy to be a keeper but it helps. It could well be argued that this is magnified in futsal given the powerful shots flying the way of the keeper and the need for the keeper to throw their body – and often their face – in the way of the ball. However, perhaps the biggest mental attribute required is in fact resilience.

Resilience

Keepers are going to mess up. The problem that keepers have is when they mess up, it often leads to a goal. Futsal is unforgiving, relentless. A keeper can make save after save, but if they drop just one clanger that is what will likely be remembered.

Mistakes are a normal part of the learning process. Even the best keepers make mistakes. It's how a keeper deals with those mistakes that can set them apart from the rest.

The good news is that resilience can be developed in training by adding stress to the session and outside of training through discussion. A coach could squeeze the space available to a keeper, add physical distractions such as a competing pivot, throw in extra movements to disrupt their peripheral vision or even ask them to perform other tasks at the same time, such as juggling a balloon. These all make training harder, meaning there'll be more negative outcomes for the keeper.

Negative Outcomes are Positive

As coaches we shouldn't demand 100 per cent success rates. Though it may create a feel-good factor amongst the team, it isn't likely to prepare them for games against top opponents. By making training hard and increasing the negative outcomes, you're more likely to develop resilient players capable of finding solutions to complex problems – thus raising their internal belief.

Away from training, discussions can take place which analyse actions that happened on court. The coach can then ask the following questions:

- What happened in that situation?
- Why did it happen?
- How can that be prevented next time?

In combination with what they have learnt from training, keepers can then begin to build a gameplan which they can refer to the next time they find themselves in a similar situation. This will allow them to think how the same outcome can be prevented from happening. With time, keepers will be able to take ownership of their actions while also developing their belief, confidence and preparedness for matches.

Leadership

The greater the ownership the keeper takes, the more likely they are to develop their leadership. By dealing with situations as they come and organising the team from the tactical information they are seeing and assessing on court, they are leading.

As the coach, it is possible to develop this leadership further. Players can be handed greater responsibility, but they can also be encouraged to challenge in a positive way. This has the added benefit of improving the whole team and not just the individual. Once players are happy with themselves, they're in a position to help others. It is because of this that mentality links well with leadership. By having a team of happy players, you're more likely to have a team of leaders.

SESSION PLANS

The following sessions have been developed by Andrew Reading to bring out in possession principles – particularly with regards to distribution. Key coaching points are detailed, along with extra information to help you get the most out of each session.

THE FITNESS BALL

ORGANISATION

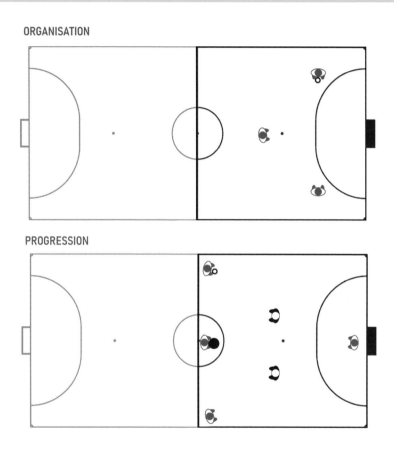

PROGRESSION

Number of Players: 1–4 goalkeepers

Equipment: Goal, balls, fitness ball

IP Objectives: Improve technical aspects of throwing and passing with timing and accuracy, speed and weight of pass, quality decision-making and peripheral vision.

ORGANISATION

Goalkeepers work in a square or triangle to develop the basics. At first, they play two balls between them, using different distribution types with both hands and feet. As the players become more comfortable, they are each given a ball. They must then work together to time their throws appropriately and in sync. This requires peripheral vision and communication. The coach can call 'change' to make the keepers change the direction they are passing in at any time. They can also make the keepers use different combinations such as roll, two-touch pass, throw to the chest.

PROGRESSIONS

- One goalkeeper sets up in goal. Another goalkeeper, or the coach, stands on the halfway line with the ball. They then play this ball into the keeper standing in goal. As soon as the keeper controls the ball, the coach then rolls a fitness ball from the halfway line toward either sideline. The keeper must look up, see the position of the fitness ball, and distribute the ball in their possession so that it hits the fitness ball before it reaches the sideline
- The spare goalkeeper or coach can feint which way they are going to roll the fitness ball
- A pivot can be added to provide distraction and disrupt the keeper's peripheral vision

COACHING POINTS

Before Phase –
- Read the position of the outfield players
- Scan for movement while assessing the speed and weight of the pass or throw

During Phase –
- Pass or throw selection
- Timing of release to moving object
- Speed and weight of pass

After Phase –
- Positioning in relation to the receiver
- Instructions to the receiver (in the initial drill)

LINKS TO FOOTBALL

When playing out from the back, the keeper needs to assess constantly changing information such as player movement (replicated by the fitness ball). How they make effective decisions based on that information can lead to effective ball retention and even create opportunities to attack.

WHITE WATER RAPIDS

FOCUS: When to Play Long and When to Play Short

ORGANISATION

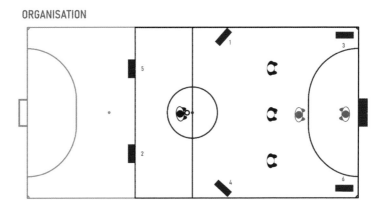

Number of Players: 1 or 2 goalkeepers

Equipment: Goal, balls, mannequins (optional), mini goals or cones to create mini gates

IP Objectives: Make the right distribution decision with the hands or feet.

OOP Objectives: Decide whether to catch, head, hold or parry.

ORGANISATION

The goalkeeper starts by facing their own goal. The coach is on the halfway line and has a ball in their hands. On the coach's call, the keeper must turn around. At the same time, the coach releases the ball and throws it toward the goalkeeper's area. The goalkeeper must react accordingly, deciding whether to catch the ball, head it clear, hold on to it or parry it.

The coach can then add another layer of complexity by reciting numbers of their choosing as the keeper makes the decision. Whatever the last number is that the coach says, this is the number of the mini goal or gate that the goalkeeper must then distribute to with quality. Don't forget the four-second rule!

PROGRESSIONS

- The coach can move along the line to change the angle of the throw
- Add a shadow pivot in to the edge of the D to complicate the decision-making process
- The shadow pivot can apply passive pressure to the keeper throughout or stay static so the keeper must work around them, encouraging mobility across the area
- Throw to the pivot to go 1v1 before making the keeper distribute with quality

COACHING POINTS
Before Phase –
- Peripheral vision: where is the pivot?
- Take up a good position from which to execute an action
- Pick up on the speed and trajectory of the pass

During Phase –
- Technique and execution of action
- Commit to the action – being half-hearted may land you in trouble
- Identify the passing line out of pressure
- Identify the final release decision and action
- Execute the distribution while on the move or under pressure

After Phase –
- Take up appropriate support position for receiver

LINKS TO FOOTBALL
Keepers have to be brave when coming to claim the ball – especially in actions such as corners or free-kicks when there are lots of bodies around them. This exercise not only mimics the decisions they need to make, but encourages them to then create an attacking opportunity with quick and effective distribution. Doing so changes the mindset of the keeper and encourages them to see themselves as a creator.

THE FOOT SELECTION BOX

FOCUS: Improving Distribution Under Pressure

ORGANISATION

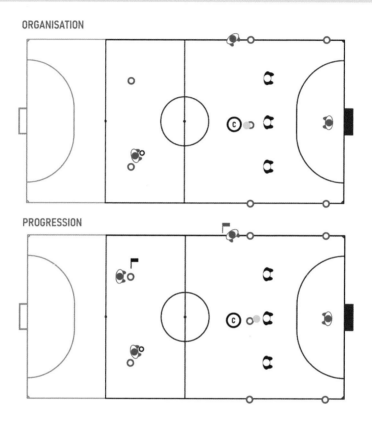

PROGRESSION

Number of Players: 4–5 goalkeepers

Equipment: Goal, balls, 3× mannequins (or visual blocks such as upright tables), tennis balls, cones, bibs

IP Objectives: Use the right technique for a range of passes with both feet, along with decision-making and perception skills.

ORGANISATION

The goalkeeper starts by facing their own goal. The coach starts behind any of the three mannequins. The practice begins when the coach rolls a tennis ball either side of the goalkeeper. As soon as the keeper spots the tennis ball in their peripheral vision they will turn. As they turn, they'll see a spare goalkeeper standing on one of the six cones with a ball. The spare goalkeeper passes or throws to the keeper, who then must search to find the second spare goalkeeper who will be standing on one of the other five cones. As this takes place, the coach rushes forward from their starting position to add pressure to the keeper. To add another layer of complexity, the second spare keeper can shout 'feet' or 'chest' to indicate where they would like to receive the pass.

PROGRESSIONS

- The coach can move along the line to change the angle of the throw
- Add a shadow pivot in to the edge of the D to complicate the decision-making process
- The shadow pivot can apply passive pressure to the keeper throughout
- Throw to the pivot to go 1v1 before making the keeper distribute with quality

COACHING POINTS

Before Phase –
- Peripheral vision: where is the tennis ball?
- Readiness to turn
- Information gathering
- Formulate a plan of action

During Phase –
- Create passing lines using the space of the area
- Pass selection: which is best?
- Deal with the oncoming pressure

After Phase –
- Take up appropriate support position for receiver
- React in transition if their distribution is poor and loses possession

LINKS TO FOOTBALL

Developing keepers to make better passing decisions enhances the build-up play of a team and makes the keeper a more potent attacker. Adding in pressure mimics an onrushing forward, helping the keeper to deal with a match situation.

OUT OF POSSESSION

Individual keepers have different strengths. The attributes discussed in these pages help them to have a variety of solutions to different problems. If any particular area is a weakness, it should be prioritized for development. As discussed, any flaw in a keeper will be picked on and brutally exposed by a competent opponent.

Shot-Stopping

To many keepers who play futsal for the first time, the movements can feel unnatural. Given the comparative narrowness of a futsal goal to an eleven-a-side goal, the techniques used to cover the goal are different. A wider goal calls for many more dives to make saves, whereas the more narrow futsal goal calls for more blocks, smothers of the ball and enlarged body shape to put off the attacker.

Keeping out shots is all to do with positioning. If a keeper is in the right place in the goal, they should only need to dive for shots that are hip-height and higher. Given this, the dive should be the last resort.

Many keepers new to futsal tend to lead with their hands when making a save. This is especially the case for keepers who have learnt their skills in football. It is a habit that needs to be changed for success in futsal.

In addition to the dive, there are a number of different saving techniques: Spanish-style blocking, Brazilian two-knee slide, split save, K save, forward kick-through, paddle. Given the unnatural movements of many, these saves will require agility, flexibility, balance – and plenty of repetition.

The Split Save

The hard surface may be a deterrent for diving, but it also presents opportunities for techniques such as sliding. The split save requires a goalkeeper to make themselves as big as possible by throwing one leg out sideways and keeping both arms out wide, ready for the hands to be adjusted to the correct height to make a save either side. This leg comes out almost at a right angle to block the low shot into the corner. It is particularly effective when scampering across goal to block a shot at the second post. Indeed, it is arguably the most efficient save in a futsal keeper's armoury.

The key instrument is the head. If the head falls back then the keeper loses their shape, so it is vital to have your head still and over your shoulders. Along with a reasonable level of core strength, this keeps the keeper's back forward and the whole torso upright. If the torso's position drops then the keeper will likely have to drop their hands back to support themselves as they fight to keep their balance. This makes it hard to then use the hands to save the ball and also makes it trickier to recover.

An essential detail of the split save is in the position of the foot of the leading leg. This should be upright. If the sole of the foot remains in contact with the floor then there'll be a lot of friction, meaning the keeper will end up fighting the floor. Instead, using the heel of the leading leg will allow the foot to slide along the floor. As a keeper, the floor is your friend!

There are two kinds of split save: splits in motion and the static split save.

Splits in motion occurs when a keeper moves across their goal and throws their body in the direction of where they anticipate the shot is about to come. It's key to assess the speed of the pass to work out the kind of shot that is likely to arrive. If the pace of the ball is slower and the keeper can keep up with the ball as it moves across the court then they may stay set with the feet and have enough time to approach the player at the second post. If, however, the ball speed is fast then the keeper should start stepping their feet over to take bigger strides across their goal and allow for a smoother transition when they move into a split.

Use the Information

Work out the speed of the ball and the positioning of the attacker to assess which save type to use.

Note the use of the lateral leg to increase coverage of the goal.

The static split save occurs when a keeper is in their set position and makes a reaction split based upon what they see.

Both the static split save and splits in motion have unique ways of recovering. For the splits in motion, the keeper's trailing leg can kick through after the initial split so you can spin on your rear to get yourself set for the second save. For the static split save, it is best to 'scissor' up. This involves getting both arms either side of the lead leg to push back up and reposition for the second save.

React Quickly

Recovering for a second save should become habitual. This can be encouraged by always making a keeper keep out a second shot immediately after the first in training. It'll teach them to react rather than sitting back and admiring the first save.

Forward Kick-Through

While the split save requires a keeper to throw their leg laterally, the forward kick-through gets them to throw their lead leg forward. It is useful for times when there is a shot in and around the keeper's feet that they have minimal reaction time to deal with. This means they do not have time to drop into a K save or use their hands. When done well, the keeper can even control where the ball goes: ideally out of play and away from the danger.

K Save/Spanish-Style Block

This is the traditional Spanish way of goalkeeping. It often happens in a 1v1 situation where the keeper comes out to reduce the angle. If the attacker has full control of the ball then the keeper needs to remain patient, waiting on their feet for the right moment to perform the K save. It is therefore a more measured, patient approach.

To select which save to make, the keeper should not only identify the attacker's level of ball control, but also their body shape and approach. The keeper must react as soon as the moment occurs. First, they must narrow the angle and play the percentages because the reaction time is minimal. If a keeper stays in goal then that gives an attacker lots of time to make their decision.

When the decision is made to drop into the K save, a keeper drops their trailing leg sideways toward the floor to create a 'long barrier'. This prevents the ball going between their legs. It is important to note that the leg should not drop the whole way to the floor, as this will make changing the position of the body harder if the attacker suddenly changes the angle of attack or makes a pass. The other leg, the one closest to the near post, remains up with the knee bent at a 90-degree angle. The chest is upright to increase the keeper's size and the hands are ready at either side with arms spread out wide.

Brazilian Two-Knee Slide

The level of control of an attacker is the key to a successful Brazilian two-knee slide. If the attacker does not have full control of the ball, the keeper should rush out and perform the save to smother the ball, attacking the ball and the player. This requires them to slide with both knees forward, meaning the attacker cannot easily strike the ball on the floor. Their chest remains up to also minimize the chance of the chip.

The Paddle

An ideal save for aerial shots. In the paddle, the keeper pushes out both hands together to push the ball to safety. Using both hands increases the surface area that the ball makes contact with, as well as the strength of connection. It is therefore a firmer, meatier way of making a save. It is often used for more powerful shots or when it is impossible to catch the ball. As a rule, it is always ideal to catch because that brings into play the possibility of starting a counter-attack.

When working with a keeper on their shot-stopping, encourage them to draw a semi-circle around their body which covers an area in which they can use their feet to save a shot. If the ball goes beyond that circle and is low, a keeper should use the split save. If the ball ends up more than double the distance of that circle away then a keeper should elect to dive or slide with their hands. At first these choices will not be natural, but by working smartly the right save selection can come innately. Soon enough, keepers will know whether or not they have time to fall into a K save.

From here, progress to working with 1v1s. Once they get out to the opponent they must decide which save to adopt. Is it a two-knee slide or do they take a more measured approach? Much of the decision will depend on the opponent's control of the ball. If they have full control then the keeper should stay set and adopt the more measured Spanish-style block, for example.

Whatever they eventually decide, they must make the decision quickly – even if it is the wrong one. There is nothing worse than a dithering goalkeeper. It makes it harder for their defenders to react and gives the attacker more opportunities. Even if they make the wrong decision, their teammates can then react accordingly.

Know The Game

All keepers should be geeks. What is meant by that is they should enjoy studying the game. That's because the better they understand the game, the better the decisions they'll be able to make.

For example, knowing which spaces need protecting and sweeping will impact the depth of a keeper's starting position. This is team dependent. If the outfield players are operating in a low block, the keeper is likely to start deeper. If the players are pressing against an opponent playing in a 4-0 that looks to draw in pressure and exploit space with forward passes over the defensive line, the keeper will likely need to adopt a higher starting position.

Most teams will attempt to hit their highest player, usually the pivot, early on. By knowing the game and understanding movements, the keeper can work out how to counteract this. Similarly, understanding the rotations an opponent does will enable a keeper to work out the areas they will look to play in. This will then help them to eliminate dangerous passes. Each team has a different way of playing, meaning each match will have different problems that require different solutions.

When sweeping, it's important for keepers to make a quick decision and commit to it. To be ready to go, they should adopt a pose similar to a runner's starting position (commonly known as the ready shape) when the ball is in the opponent's half and they are sweeping and protecting their half. Their balance and momentum must be in the right direction. If the ball is in their defensive half then the keeper should be in the set position so they are able to deal with shots. This change from the ready shape to the set shape takes place when an opponent gets within 10m of the goal.

If they elect to stay in goal and the ball does reach the opponent's pivot, the keeper needs to analyse further to see what tends to happen next. Are there supporting runs or will the pivot attempt to turn and shoot? Does the team like to get a player on the second post? Will the keeper's teammates drop low or stay high when that happens? If the keeper communicates well, will it be possible to stop the pass to the pivot at source? Being able to answer these questions aids starting position along with save selection. Giving keepers the confidence to change a team's gameplan and improvise if needed can lead to success.

SESSION PLANS

The following sessions have been developed by Andrew Reading to bring out of possession principles to life. Key coaching points are

Organisation in action.

detailed, along with extra information to help you get the most out of each session.

Bear in mind that these sessions can be enhanced by bringing in top players to improve the quality of shooting and feinting, along with incorporating specialist players such as pivots with good game understanding. The unpredictable nature of quality players will only improve the keepers – even if it does reduce their success rate (a fantastic psychological benefit to increase resilience). As a result, the keepers will have to deal with movements that are realistic to matches and similar outcomes.

There's also a social benefit of keepers mixing with their teammates.

However, if it's not an option to add players into the session, it is also beneficial to have keepers mimic these roles themselves. By playing as a pivot, a second post striker or taking part in a 1v1 as the attacking player, keepers will understand how attackers think when they go up against keepers. This then helps them to know what they can expect when in goal and facing attackers. By taking on these roles, keepers also get to fine-tune their passing and control.

STABILIZING THE SPLIT

FOCUS: Developing the Split Save

ORGANISATION

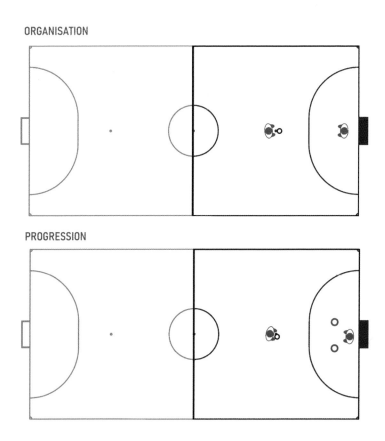

PROGRESSION

Number of Players: 1–4 goalkeepers

Equipment: Goal, balls, tennis balls, cones

OOP Objectives: Analyse the split save technique and understand how to maintain the shape.

ORGANISATION

The goalkeeper begins in the final split save shape with their heel on the floor and their toe facing upwards. Their opposite knee is flexed with their gluteus maximus on the floor and their head over their shoulders. Their arms are extended either side of their body.

The coach then throws a futsal ball for the keeper in the position, who catches and returns while holding the position. Next up, the coach throws a tennis ball to add differentiation and encourage the keeper to use their hands more.

After this, the keeper goes onto both knees and the coach bounces a tennis ball or ball toward the goal. The keeper should then straighten the leading leg with their toe facing upwards, using the heel to slide it across the goal. If possible, they then catch and throw the ball back.

The keeper will then have to link these two movements together by starting on both knees and sliding into the final split save shape when they catch the ball. Once they are comfortable with this, they should take a standing start before getting into the final split save position. Importantly, their opposite knee should be in contact with the surface. Using a training disc or cone under the opposite knee can aid this movement.

Early movements should be made in a steady, controlled manner to emphasize the full movements and maintain physical integrity.

PROGRESSIONS

- As above but finish by picking up cones and moving into a standing set position
- The coach shoots low to one side rather than bouncing a ball to the keeper. This can be progressed further with a mid-to-low shot that brings the hands into play for the save
- A goalkeeper keeps a cone in either hand and makes saves just with their legs. They then place these cones on the floor in front of them after each save to show the coach they have full control of their split save
- Add a recovery using a scissor action with the legs and arms to teach the importance of reacting to second shots
- Add a physical element by making the keeper recover through a set of cones after making the save, then returning to their goal to make a second save

COACHING POINTS

Before Phase –

- Adopt ready and set positions at all stages

During Phase –

- Head needs to stay forward
- Toes facing up
- Use the heel to slide
- Keep arms extended out wide
- Use hands and legs to make saves
- Pick up the height and line of the shot early

After Phase –

- Recover using the scissors to get into a ready position again

LINKS TO FOOTBALL

Shots where the keeper has a minimal reaction time require them to become as big as possible to minimize the area the attacker has to shoot at. By teaching a keeper a split save, they can use it to cover a great area with a great speed, improving their save percentage in football.

SPLIT OR KICK?

FOCUS: Decision-Making when Saving at Speed

ORGANISATION

PROGRESSION

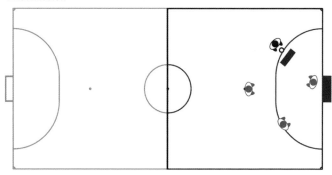

Number of Players: 3+ goalkeepers

Equipment: Goal, balls, a visual barrier that the ball can be passed under so that the keeper sees the ball very late (for example a bridge)

OOP Objectives: To improve the speed of action in the split save or forward kick-through, identifying when to perform the action with sufficient reaction time, stride pattern and transition.

ORGANISATION
The coach starts with the ball. They either shoot, pass through the visual barrier to the spare keeper at the second post to finish, or drive around the barrier to create a 1v1. They must finish with three touches while the spare keeper must finish in two touches. The keeper decides whether to use the split save or forward kick-through, while if the ball goes to the second post they can attempt to intercept, and if the coach goes for the 1v1 they can block.

PROGRESSIONS
- Add a third outfield player (or spare keeper) who can also receive a pass from the coach and shoot with no more than two touches
- This third player can also drive into the area to score (with no more than three touches and unable to play to the second post finisher)

- The third player can pass to the second post finisher
- The third player can be used as a second shot or second phase action from 10m

COACHING POINTS
Before Phase –
- Adopt ready and set position
- Protect the front post
- Be aware of the other attackers

During Phase –
- Split save in first phase and at the second post
- Decision-making at the second post – which save to use
- Perform the forward kick-through save when necessary
- Move across goal effectively, transitioning into splits

After Phase –
- Quickly recover for the second phase
- Distribute the ball effectively if able to catch

LINKS TO FOOTBALL
In goalmouth scrambles or set-pieces, the keeper often has little time to react. This exercise develops saving techniques that can be adopted with minimal reaction time while also emphasizing a quick recovery for action in the second phase.

THE THREE-GOAL GAME

FOCUS: Improve the Parrying Technique and Saving at the Second Post

ORGANISATION

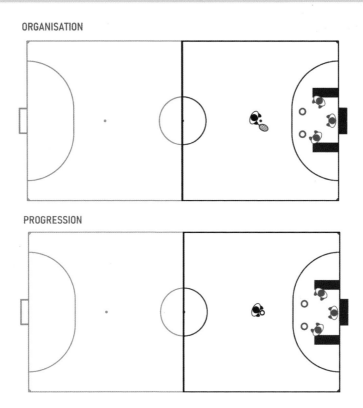

PROGRESSION

Number of Players: 3 goalkeepers and a coach

Equipment: 3× goals, balls, tennis balls, tennis racket, cones

OOP Objectives: Effectively save hard shots that cannot be caught, developing the body shape to generate momentum and power in the parry.

ORGANISATION

The coach starts at the 10m penalty spot and fires tennis balls either into the ground or directly at the keeper, who must parry them. To the sides of the main goal, two keepers stand protecting their own goal. When the first keeper parries a ball to either side, these other keepers must first touch the green cone (this can also be a punchbag for a different kind of pre-movement) then recover to make a 'second post' save from the parried ball. The first keeper is attempting to successfully parry the balls into the second and third goals, while the second and third keepers attempt to keep the balls out.

To work on specific areas and saves, the coach can perform this exercise by sectioning off parts of the goal (for example, removing the top half of the goal to keep the focus on low saves, or removing the bottom half to focus on the paddle).

161

PROGRESSIONS

- The coach moves closer and does the same practice but with futsal balls instead of tennis balls
- If the ball is parried and remains in the area then the three keepers can attempt to finish in each other's goal until the action is complete
- If the ball is parried back out to the coach then they can hit a second shot

COACHING POINTS

Before Phase –

- Awareness and peripheral vision
- Read cues and triggers of the ball striker

During Phase –

- Save into safe areas
- Improvisation

- Effective parry save
- Second post save

After Phase –

- Reaction to the second phase

LINKS TO FOOTBALL

Reaction saves in the 6yd box with quick footwork and secondary saves are a vital part of any football goalkeeper's armoury. In addition to this, this exercise teaches keepers the importance of getting a good connection behind the ball. This is especially important to minimize the danger of rebounds and encourage keepers to push the ball into safe areas from where it is hard to score.

RAPID BLOCK

FOCUS: Recognize and Engage the Block as Quickly as Possible

ORGANISATION

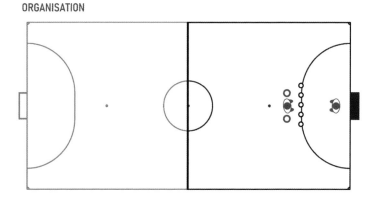

PROGRESSION

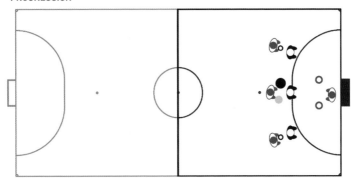

Number of Players: Goalkeeper and 3 players (including the coach)

Equipment: Goal, balls, tennis ball cones, mannequin

OOP Objectives: Apply and execute the correct block or spread save with timing of approach, appropriate positioning and peripheral vision.

ORGANISATION

Five futsal balls are set up on the edge of the D. The exercise starts with the keeper approaching the set of balls. The coach stands behind the balls and can then elect to shoot any of the five. The keeper must move into line with the ball that is struck and make a K shape save before recovering for the next shot.

At any point, the coach can throw a tennis ball for the keeper to make a hand save. The practice ends when all five balls have been shot.

PROGRESSIONS
- The keeper starts by facing their own goal. The coach stands behind a mannequin and throws a tennis ball past the keeper. Once the keeper sees the ball in their peripheral vision, they turn and touch the green cone to their side. This triggers a player to drive in a 1v1 against the keeper. The player has three touches to score and the keeper must reposition themselves to block the ball carrier. The ball carrier can

come from either side of the mannequin, or even be the coach.
- Remove the cones and allow the opposite player the choice to attack the second post. The goalkeeper then has to either block the 1v1 or protect the goal with awareness of the second post runner. If a second post run is made then the ball carrier is limited to two touches and they can only pass or shoot.

COACHING POINTS
Before Phase –
- Peripheral vision
- Appropriate starting position in terms of height and angles

During Phase –
- Turn to set and gather the information to make a rapid decision
- Identify the 1v1 or second post movement
- Speed and line of approach
- Correct technique to block, spread or save

After Phase –
- Recover to set position

LINKS TO FOOTBALL
1v1 situations are critical in football. For a defensive team they are high risk. Becoming proficient in these situations and learning to smother the ball quickly can help a keeper keep the ball out of their net.

BLOCKING THE ONE

FOCUS: Blocking and Spreading in and around the D

ORGANISATION

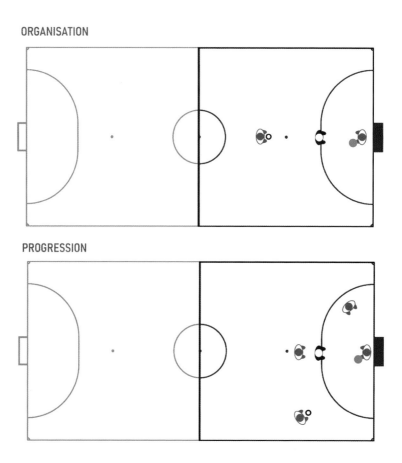

PROGRESSION

Number of Players: Goalkeeper and 2 players (including the coach)

Equipment: Goal, balls, mannequin, balloons

OOP Objectives: Identify 1v1 situations, then execute the correct block or spread save with appropriate approach and timing, holding the shape to recover back to goal.

ORGANISATION
The coach begins the practice by serving a ball into a pivot player, who has three touches to

turn or roll the mannequin and finish at goal. While this happens, the keeper is juggling a balloon in the air. When the keeper identifies the 1v1 in their peripheral vision (once the pivot has turned) they must hit the balloon high in the air and then advance quickly to engage in a 1v1 in and around the D. After they have made the save, the keeper then attempts to recover the balloon before it touches the floor. Here it is ideal for the keeper to move backwards while their shoulders face the court for positional recovery. If they find this too challenging at first, it is most important they maintain the block position when attempting to retrieve the balloon before progressing to moving backwards. The coach also has the option of incorporating a second shot for the keeper to recover to.

PROGRESSIONS
- The coach or player who serves the ball into the pivot can support the pivot for a set and shot or to go 1v1
- As above but the third player has to move to the second post to create more decisions for the keeper
- If the second post option is available, the ball carrier can shoot or pass to the second post (with a maximum of two touches)
- If there is no second post option then the ball carrier can shoot (maximum of two touches) or create a 1v1 (maximum of three touches)

COACHING POINTS
Before Phase –
- Watch the opponent while juggling the balloon – peripheral vision
- Approach of the 1v1

During Phase –
- Identify 1v1 from game information
- Recognize the level of control the pivot has on the ball
- Correct line of approach
- Execute the correct save with the correct technique

After Phase –
- Recover to goal aware of any new danger while also searching for the balloon

LINKS TO FOOTBALL
Quickly squeezing the attackers' space can lead them to panic and gives an advantage to the keeper in 1v1 situations. This exercise emphasizes the need to be able to spring into action and quickly confront danger. The keeper therefore recognizes danger and reacts accordingly. Though this is focused on blocks and shot-stopping, it can just as easily mirror a keeper's need to react quickly to a ball over the top that breaks the last line of defence.

DEFENDING THE HALF

FOCUS: Protect the Half as a Sweeper Keeper with Transition

ORGANISATION

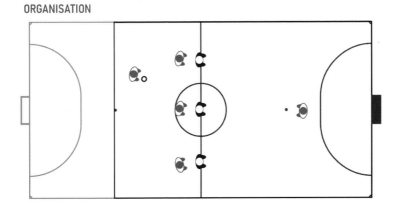

Number of Players: 2+ goal keepers and 3+ outfield players

Equipment: Goal, balls, mannequins, cones

OOP Objectives: Understand the importance of positioning in relation to the ball, working out how to protect and defend the space and when to protect the goal.

ORGANISATION

The coach stands behind the mannequins. There are players behind each of the three mannequins on the halfway line. These players can make runs to feint and receive a pass in the attacking half. The goalkeeper must protect the space or the passing lines into the attackers. The coach then plays a variety of attacking passes into the half, which challenge the keeper's positioning and create different situations for them to deal with. The ball receiver has a maximum of three touches with which to score.

PROGRESSIONS

- Players on the mannequin can drive out with a ball
- Once the keeper has control of the ball the other mannequin players become forward passes in transition
- Add bibs for extra complexity: if a player holds a bib in the air then that means they are marked and not available for the transition pass

- Once the coach has played the pass they can then become an extra defender

COACHING POINTS
Before Phase –
- Be ready to sprint out or recover
- High start position
- Body shape to enable the forward sprint
- Reading of the game information: where are the hips pointing, which are the dangerous runs, where is the available space?

During Phase –
- Decision of whether to advance to sweep
- Hold the ball and distribute or kick it out to stop the danger
- Use of the feet
- Engage in the 1v1 with a block or sweep

After Phase –
- Recover to the goal
- Pass or distribute in positive transition

LINKS TO FOOTBALL
Sweeper keepers are an important part of the modern game. They allow football teams to defend with a high line. Alert to the danger, they 'sweep' up any dangerous through balls that cut through the last line of defence. This exercise reinforces the need to be alert to danger.

KEEPER MAYHEM

FOCUS: Stay Focused in Quick Shot-Stopping across Low, Medium and High Saves

ORGANISATION

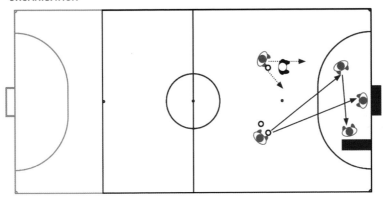

Number of Players: 2 goalkeepers and 2+ players

Equipment: 2× goals, balls, mannequins, cones

OOP Objectives: Execute the correct save techniques under pressure, making second post saves and selecting the best action most appropriate to the defending scenario.

ORGANISATION

The practice starts with the second post player and the keeper passing a ball between them using the soles of the feet. This second post player can decide to shoot at the second goal whenever they want, meaning the second keeper must be alert to the danger.

After this shot, the first goalkeeper must touch the second post of their own goal and then recover, ready for a shot from the coach from distance. They must then attempt to parry this shot into the second goalkeeper's goal. Following this action, the coach then passes the ball to the player on the second post, who can shoot into either goal.

Finally, a third player who starts behind a mannequin waits for any second phase shots and finishes with a maximum of two touches or drives into the area with a maximum of three touches before finishes at either goal. If the ball remains live in this phase then any player or goalkeeper involved can attempt to score in any goal. After that action, the round is finished.

COACHING POINTS

Before Phase –
- Ready and start positions
- Perceptional awareness of cues and triggers
- Set positions and start positions in relation to each ball

During Phase –
- Different types of shot-stopping for the type of shot (low, medium and high)
- Timing and approach to get closer to the ball in relation to the speed of pass and first touch of the attacker

- Decision to use a block, split save, parry or second post save depending on the situation

After Phase –
- Recover to reset position in goal ready for the next phase
- Identify the next attack or 1v1

LINKS TO FOOTBALL
Keepers must regularly make multiple saves in and around the area with minimal reaction time. This exercise teaches them different techniques to improve their success rates while also working on reaction times and agility.

IN SUMMARY

Free-thinking, independent keepers are the best kind of futsal keepers. As a coach, encourage innovation, spontaneity and, most importantly, resilience. Promoting constant analysis and evaluation leads to steady improvements and actionable training plans.

Remember, a goalkeeper is so much more than a shot-stopper. They're an organiser, a creator, the last line of defence, and in some cases a scorer of goals. They should be equally confident with the ball at their feet as they are at saving shots. When that's the case, the team benefits greatly.

Conclusion

Futsal: the fast, furious and fun game that's taking the world by storm. To some it's football on steroids; to others it's a fantastic standalone sport. In this book you've been introduced to the key concepts and requirements to play futsal at every level, from the grassroots to the elite.

Central to these concepts is a game model. Yours may look different to the one that we shared. You may have different priorities or challenges. However, once you build from that very model the rest will be put into place.

The sessions outlined in these pages are frameworks for you to put your own stamp on. It may be that you wish to use an in possession session to work on defenders pressing, or perhaps you wonder what it'd look like if the defenders adopted a low block and whether that'd create new challenges for your attackers.

The beauty of futsal is that because it's such a quick game, scenarios constantly change. New tactics and styles of play are constantly emerging. As sport science takes a greater hold on the sport and players become fitter, further innovations are just around the corner. The game is fast now, and it's only likely to become faster – and even more physical.

The coach's job is to guide players with key principles and give them the tools of the trade. How they use those tools is down to them.

A fast and furious game of high emotions.

Futsal is a game of decisions and the coach cannot possibly guide every one of these from the sideline; instead, the ownership has to be on the player. The framework from which this ownership comes, however, is the coach's responsibility.

PERCEPTION > DECISION > ACTION

Futsal is great fun to play and great fun to coach. Keep enjoyment central to your sessions and the benefits will be broad.

GLOSSARY

Block – standing in front of an opponent to prevent them from moving forward

Box – a method of defending or attacking that mirrors a box shape, typically with two players forward and two players back

Brazilian two-knee slide – a method of saving a shot where the keeper slides with both knees on the floor to smother a shot, attacking the player and ball with their movement

Choreographed movement – a rehearsed play where players perform set movements to create and then exploit space in possession

Closing the middle – preventing the opponent from passing balls forward into the middle of the court between defenders

Combination play – set movements between two attackers, such as wall passes

Compactness – a defensive style where players set up close to each other to deny the opponent space

Defensive lines – how deep players position themselves on court (from 1–5)

Diamond – a defensive system with one player at the back, two wingers and one at the top, mirroring a diamond. This tends to be positioned with the highest player in a team's own half

Dualities – movements between two players

Emergency defending – last-ditch defending where players typically throw their bodies in the way of shots. In these moments, tactics go out the window and players do anything within the laws of the game to stop the opponent from scoring

Exchanging – passing an opponent onto a teammate to defend as they move through the court

False pivot – the player at the top of the court who then comes back into the main rotations between players

Feinting – disguising one's movements. This could be pretending to run forward, then doubling back, for example

Finish the action – making sure that an offensive action either reaches its intended outcome or goes out of play to prevent the counter-attack

Fix – the deepest lying player

Floating player – a player who plays for whichever team is in possession (can also be solely used as a defender)

Fly goalkeeper – when the goalkeeper leaves their goal and moves higher up the court to create a momentary overload

Follow – a defender moving after their attacker, common in a player-to-player system

Forward kick-through – a method of saving a shot where the keeper throws a leg forward to kick the ball to safety

Helping pass – passing into a teammate and following that pass to receive a touch to either side of that same teammate

High press – an aggressive method of winning the ball by playing high in the opponent's half

Inverted – in the opposite position. This tends to relate to left-footers playing on the right-hand-side of the court and vice versa

Jump – moving as a defender from one opponent to the next, often performed over a distance of fewer than 5m

K save – also know as the **Spanish-style block**. Here, a keeper performs a long barrier with chest upright and arms outstretched in situations where they need to take a measured approach

Lines of defence – the number of horizontal lines across a court created by defenders that opponents must get through before finishing

Low block – a method of defending where the team stays close to their own goal, with the main aim of denying space in dangerous areas

Overload – a situation where one team has more players than the other

Paddle – a method of saving an aerial shot by pushing both hands together and beating away the ball

Paired movements – set moves between two players to create opportunities

Parallel pass – a pass down the line to an oncoming teammate, often lifted slightly off the court to reduce the pace of the ball

Passing lines – imaginary lines between the passer and any possible receiver

Penetrating – a pass or movement, often forward, that compromises an opponent

Pivot – the furthest forward player, similar to a number 9 in football

Player-to-player – a defensive system where defenders follow their opponent tightly. Often known as man-to-man

Pockets of space – areas between defenders where attackers can receive passes

Powerplay – when the goalkeeper leaves their goal untended and plays in the offensive half to create a 5v4 overload

Press breaker – a set movement to create space when opponents are pressing high

Rotations – movements between players to create space

Russian four – substituting all four players on court at once

Scanning – checking over one's shoulders to build up a 360-degree view of the court

Scoop – a passing method where the foot lifts the ball from underneath to 'scoop' it into the air

Screen – standing in front of an opponent so they cannot see what is happening

Slow play – a pattern of play that happens at low intensity, such as a pass. This is a trigger to press or a chance to intercept

Spear throw – an overarm goalkeeper's technique to distribute to a player at a mid-to-long distance, such as a pivot

Split save – a method of saving a shot that requires the keeper to throw their leading leg sideways

Stabbed – a type of pass similar to a chip, but firmer, flatter and executed with the front of the foot/toe area

Swazz – a goalkeeper's technique to distribute at pace to a player a medium distance away

The D – the goalkeeper's 6m area

Transition – moving from one situation to another, such as defence to attack on the counter-attack

Traps – allowing the opponent to play in a certain direction in order to win the ball back with an overload

Triggers – visual cues that present clues as to the action that is about to take place

Underload – a situation where one team has fewer players than the other

Wall pass – a pass between two players, typically where a winger plays the ball into the middle of the court and then runs forward to receive the return pass, essentially bouncing the ball off a teammate

Winger – the player/s who play at the side of the court

Zonal – a defensive system where players hold their position and do not follow opponents as they move through the court

ACKNOWLEDGEMENTS

I would like to take this opportunity to thank all the players and staff I have worked with over the years from club and country alike, especially to my closest support staff with the Senior England National Team.

There's also Ian Bateman, James Ellis and Graeme Dell who are not only trusted friends, but also great mentors and challengers.

I would also like to thank all the key contributors to the book and particularly Seth. We wanted to share how futsal is not only an amazing grassroots game and development tool for football, but also a high-level performance sport in its own right.

Michael Skubala

Many top futsal people have helped with this book. Juan Tapia Owens, an exceptional coach at Bloomsbury, helped us with the designs. James Barlow and Joao Almeida, both excellent coaches, provided feedback along with Jamie Fahey, while Andrew Reading shared his deep knowledge in the goalkeeping chapter.

When it comes to writing, I have countless people to thank for allowing me to write the books that I want to. I'd like to pick out two in particular: Ian Ridley, my mentor who gave me my first opportunity in writing, and the Gaffer, Nick Walters, my literary agent at David Luxton Associates.

It's also been fantastic to work with the wider team at Crowood.

Seth Burkett

INDEX

Effective
SPORTS COACHING
A Practical Guide

Alan Lynn

Soccer
Drills

A
Guide
for all
Levels
of
Ability

David Smith

ISBN: 978 1 84797 194 4

ISBN: 978 1 84797 916 2

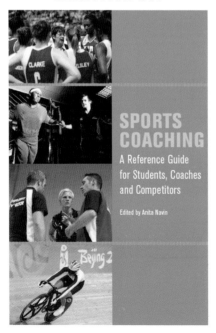

SPORTS COACHING
A Reference Guide
for Students, Coaches
and Competitors

Edited by Anita Navin

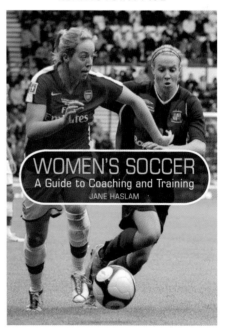

WOMEN'S SOCCER
A Guide to Coaching and Training
JANE HASLAM

ISBN: 978 1 84797 193 7

ISBN: 978 1 84797 221 7